THE GLASS OF VISION

THE
GLASS OF VISION

BY

AUSTIN FARRER

DOCTOR OF DIVINITY AND
FELLOW OF TRINITY COLLEGE, OXFORD

Now we see through a glass darkly
1 Corinthians, xiii, 12

dacre press
westminster

FIRST PUBLISHED 1948
REPRINTED 1958 AND 1966

DACRE PRESS: A. AND C. BLACK LTD
4, 5 AND 6 SOHO SQUARE LONDON W.I

PRINTED IN GREAT BRITAIN
BY NOVELLO AND COMPANY LIMITED LONDON W.I

CONTENTS

CONTENTS

PREFACE

The lectures which follow are no more than a modest attempt to state what I do, in fact, think about the relation borne to one another by three things—the sense of metaphysical philosophy, the sense of scriptural revelation, and the sense of poetry. Scripture and metaphysics are equally my study, and poetry is my pleasure. These three things rubbing against one another in my mind, seem to kindle one another, and so I am moved to ask how this happens. I would not dream of undertaking to give an adequate treatment of such a question. Perhaps, after each of the three subjects of my interest had claimed a great volume to itself, a fourth volume (but I should have broken down long before) might begin to draw them into relation with one another. If we were never to say anything unless we said everything, we should all be best advised to keep our lips sealed: but we are all vain enough to think that if we express within a limited compass what in fact interests us, it may have the luck to interest our indulgent friends. The limited compass is happily prescribed to me by the course of eight lectures allowed to a Bampton Lecturer. Here is a conveniently narrow vessel in which to mix together my three ingredients. Since any interest the experiment may have consists in a combination of things we have often considered apart, the smallness of scale may be a positive advantage—the unity will be less likely to get lost in the detail.

I fear that in touching so many and great themes with the boldness of treatment required for a lecture, I have produced something unscholarly and impressionistic. It is not only that the style may be rhetorical, for as to that, perhaps the reader will remember that lectures are, in fact, rhetoric. It is much more that there are many inconsistences in statement between one lecture and another, and it seems too much to ask of the reader that he should imagine for himself how I would have reduced them if I had written a full-scale scholastic treatise.

But I am most penitent of all for the seeming arrogance with which I have pronounced on the form of scientific and metaphysical thought, when I am very ignorant of the first, and too entramelled in the second to get it into focus. What I have said I have only said to give a broad impression relevant to the purpose I had in view: to speak of scientific thinking only in an aspect of it which contrasts with metaphysical thought; and then, no doubt, with gross exaggeration of the contrast. To generalize about the form of natural science is really absurd; every science must be allowed its own form: at the most we could arrange the sciences in a sort of scale, from the more rigidly mathematical at the one end, to the more humane and historical at the other. Let me repeat, then, that I say what I say about the characteristically scientific procedure for no other purpose but to raise a discussion about metaphysics by way of contrast. I am more concerned to say that metaphysics *is not* this than to say that any particular scientific procedure *is* just this.

In the third lecture I have used by way of illustration the Trinitarian symbolism of St. John's Revelation. The reader who is acquainted with the commentaries on that book will know that a different account of these symbols, and especially of the Seven Spirits of God, has often been preferred, and so he will be likely to complain that my citation is a piece of arbitrary and unsupported dogmatism. I would not have dogmatized if I had thought that the interpretation was open to serious doubt. I have defended it at length in a study of the Apocalypse which will be published, I hope, not long after these lectures appear.

My debts are to such obvious sources for the most part that there will be no real fraud in leaving them unacknowledged; but I would like to mention M. Gabriel Marcel, from whose *Être et Avoir* I have lifted the distinction between problems and mysteries repeated, I dare say with much distortion, in my fourth lecture.

It is the privilege of the Bampton Lecturer to commemorate from the pulpit before every lecture the Reverend John Bampton, Canon of Salisbury; recalling, it may be, with some awe the river of good doctrine which through so long a time has flowed into learned ears from that munificent source. Now here are the exact provisions of his testament:

'. . . I give and bequeath my Lands and Estates to the Chancellor, Masters and Scholars of the University of Oxford for ever, to have and to hold all and singular the said Lands or Estates upon trust, and to the intents and purposes hereinafter mentioned; that is to say, I will and appoint that the Vice-Chancellor of the University of Oxford for the time being shall take and receive all the rents, issues, and profits thereof, and (after all taxes, reparations, and necessary deductions made) that he pay all the remainder to the endowment of eight Divinity Lecture Sermons, to be established for ever in the said University, and to be performed in the manner following:

'I direct and appoint that, upon the first Tuesday in Easter Term, a Lecturer be yearly chosen by the Heads of Colleges only, and by no others, in the room adjoining to the Printing-House, between the hours of ten in the morning and two in the afternoon, to preach eight Divinity Lecture Sermons, the year following, at St. Mary's in Oxford, between the commencement of the last month in the Lent Term and the end of the third week in Act Term.

'Also I direct and appoint, that the eight Divinity Lecture Sermons shall be preached upon either of the following subjects—to confirm and establish the Christian Faith, and to confute all heretics and schismatics—upon the divine authority of the holy Scriptures—upon the authority of the writings of the primitive Fathers, as to the faith and practice of the primitive Church—upon the Divinity of our Lord and

Saviour Jesus Christ—upon the Divinity of the Holy Ghost—upon the Articles of the Christian Faith, as comprehended in the Apostles' and the Nicene Creeds.

'Also I direct, that thirty copies of the eight Divinity Lecture Sermons shall always be printed, within two months after they are preached; and one copy shall be given to the Chancellor of the University, and one copy to the Head of every College, and one copy to the Mayor of the city of Oxford, and one copy to be put into the Bodleian library; and the expense of printing them shall be paid out of the revenue of the Land or Estates given for establishing the Divinity Lecture Sermons; and the Preacher shall not be paid, nor be entitled to the revenue, before they are printed.

'Also I direct and appoint, that no person shall be qualified to preach the Divinity Lecture Sermons, unless he hath taken the degree of Master of Arts at least, in one of the two Universities of Oxford or Cambridge; and that the same person shall never preach the Divinity Lecture Sermons twice.'

Not again, says the wise testator. But, *O si melius*!

Oxford
June 1948

I

That which may be known of God is manifest among men, for God hath manifested it unto them. For his invisible attributes since the creation of the world are clearly seen, being perceived through the things that are made, even his everlasting power and deity. ROMANS, I. 19

The subject of these lectures is the form of divine truth in the human mind: and I begin today with the distinctive character of supernatural and revealed truth. For the truth of which I have principally to speak is not simply truth about God, it is revealed truth about God; and God himself has revealed it. So we believe: and in so believing we suppose that we exalt this truth, as something above what our faculties could reach; as something we could not know unless God himself declared it. Our intention is not to make truth as narrow as the Church which professes it, but as high as the God who proclaims it. There is indeed, we say, a truth about God which human reason can discover; and man might have supposed it to be the highest he could know, had it not been that God himself had spoken a higher truth to him.

Since revealed truth is exalted by comparison with natural truth, we are disconcerted to hear some Christian philosophers attack the whole basis of distinction between the two, equating revelation and reason, so far as either is able to speak truly of God. The instinct of our faith reacts against such an equation, and inclines us to look into its credentials. The equation of reason and revelation is, we find, supposed to be proved by two propositions.

The first is this: If we believe in God at all, it is absurd and impious to imagine that we can find him out by our own reason, without his being first active in revealing himself to us. Therefore all our discovery of him is his self-manifestation, and all rational theology is revealed theology.

And this is the second proposition: If God does reveal himself to us, we cannot acknowledge or master what he reveals without the use of our reason. Therefore all his self-manifestation is also our discovery of him, and all revealed theology is rational theology.

The first proposition, assuming reason, proves revelation: the second, assuming revelation, proves reason. We are intended to add the two together and establish the joint conclusion that, wherever there is knowledge of God, both factors operate: man reasons, and God reveals. We need not of course conclude that the proportion between the two factors is everywhere the same. In the wide and continuous field of human experience we shall find places at which God's operation appears more personal and more striking, and man's 'reason' has more the character of simple recognition. Again we shall find places at which God's operation is less evident or less clear, and man's reason must be consciously strained in the effort to apprehend or to interpret it. Such differences there are admitted to be, but they are not admitted to be differences of principle. Indeed, to distinguish between natural and revealed theology is positively misleading; it would be better to substitute other distinctions: say the distinction between a theology based on God's action in the general laws of nature, and a theology based on God's action in particular historical fact—in the lives, let us say, of prophets and saints. It would be more significant on this shewing to call Christianity an historical religion than to call it a revealed religion.

Such is the argument. In proceeding to discuss it, we begin by observing that the two propositions on which it stands are flat platitudes, which can scarcely have been ever contested. Who has supposed that God can be found out without his own previous act of willing self-manifestation? Or who has supposed that revealed truth can be acknowledged without any use of our rational faculties? Is it really likely that a pair of incontrovertible truisms have strength to overthrow a doctrine long maintained by philosophers and saints? One would hesitate to think so. It is not, in fact, the substance of traditional doctrine that the two propositions assail, but simply the title by which it has been frequently and infelicitously called. 'Reason and Revelation' is a current description, but a bad description, for the antithesis we have to discuss. We ought to say '*Natural* Reason and *Supernatural* Revelation', and we ought to throw the emphasis on the adjectives rather than upon the nouns. We have not to distinguish between God's action and ours, but between two phases of God's action—his supernatural action, and his action by way of nature. It is difficult to see how anything resembling Christianity can survive the denial of this distinction. For Christianity is faith in Christ, and Christ is God acting not by way of nature, but supernaturally. If you reduce Christ to a part of God's natural action, is he Christ any longer?

Let us first consider God's self-revelation by way of nature. To a theist, everything which happens in the world reveals God acting through his creatures, or, to put it otherwise, it reveals the creatures acting as themselves the effect of the Creator's act. For this reason the creatures have traditionally been called 'second causes', and God the 'first cause' of every action. The creatures, all together, make up the realm of Nature. Human minds, being themselves creatures, are parts of Nature in the sense here understood. It is particularly necessary to observe this, because German idealism has popularized the distinction between Nature and Spirit, a distinction which exempts the human spirit from the realm of nature. Let every man use words in the way best suited to make his meaning plain. For our present purpose we define Nature in such a sense that the activities of human spirit, of intellect, that is to say, and will, are parts of nature. For intelligence and voluntary choice are certainly the natural endowments of

3

man. Without them human nature would not be human nature, but some other thing.

By Nature, then, we mean the universe of creatures or the sum of second causes, including man. By including man in nature we do not subject him to the iron rule of natural law, or otherwise pretend that he is something lower than he is. For us, nature is not a machine operated by divine controls; it is a multitude of interplaying forces, sustained in being by the Father of Life. Some natural activities operate in close accord with fixed patterns, others more freely. Nature is not natural because it is bound; it is natural because it is the real operation of second causes, whether they are bound or free. Men are free, or rather, they are just as free as they discover themselves to be; but their actions, in being free, do not cease to be natural; it is their nature to be free, and in exercising their freedom they express their nature. Not that a man is free to be anything you like: he cannot exercise the activities of an angel, nor even the activities of an eagle. He can only exercise his own, those, that is to say, which belong to his nature, and to his place in the total nature.

When we speak, therefore, of God's operation by way of nature, we refer to those activities which he, their first cause, enables the multitude of second causes to perform, in accordance with the various natures he has assigned them. What happens, then, when man knows God by nature, by his natural reason? We must answer that both the object and the subject of such knowledge are supplied by God; by God, that is, working in the way of nature. Any example will serve to make this plain. Let us take the most hackneyed of all—Aristotle reasoning his way from stellar motions to his Prime Mover Unmoved. (It may well be that his reasoning is wholly invalid: it will still serve for our example.) The object he studies is the stellar motions, and these motions are the activities of second causes, of the energies which compose the bodies of the stars. And they, in moving, express the activity of their first cause, God. So much for the object of Aristotle's study. As to the subject, it is Aristotle's own mind; itself a second cause, exerting a power of speculation continually derived from God, the first cause and archetypal mind. Aristotle, who had, indeed, scarcely the rudiments of what we call theistic belief, chose to concentrate his attention on the activity of God revealed in the stars he studied, rather than upon the activity of God revealed in his own mind as he studied the stars. But in principle either path can be taken. We can ascend from second to first cause either on the side of the subject or of the object. Aristotle was himself aware that the human subject, speculating as he speculated, was exerting an act not so much human as divine.

What do we learn from the example we have taken? That the most aridly theoretical speculation, the typical case of rational theologizing, is to be attributed to the divine initiative: to God working by way of nature, God who wills to display himself in the stars, God who wills to elevate a philosopher's mind along the paths of astral contemplation. There is no question of the philosopher's finding God out, as a child may find his father out, unwilling or unaware. God may be in some sense a jealous God, but his jealousy is not this. He is not unwilling to be known, but only (if so) unwilling that, knowing him, we should attribute the achievement to ourselves. In apprehending the Creator through the creature, the philosopher has no cause to boast: he simply consents not to frustrate a principal purpose of his natural being, when the way has opened for him to fulfil it.

But if, in the case we have taken, there is no question of denying the divine initiative, equally there is no question of asserting an action of God outside the bounds of nature. The stars and the philosopher were both exerting their proper forces. There is nothing supernatural about Aristotle's enlightenment.

There are, I know, many people who will listen to a discussion such as this with some impatience. 'When', they say, 'the religious mind insists that God is not to be known with-

out his revealing initiative, it is not to be put off with philosophic generalities about the universal operation of *Deus sive
Natura*. To tell us that what we call nature can be called God
achieving his ends by way of nature, really alters nothing.
What we mean is that God is not to be known by us unless he
reveals himself *personally*. Aristotle was, you say, quite unaware of God's personally communicating to him anything.
Very well: in that case we shall be inclined to say one or other
of two things. We are willing to suppose that Aristotle's mind
responded to no personal divine communication, in which
case the First Mover he called God will have had no truly
divine character, but will be an idol of the philosophic
mind. Alternatively we are willing to suppose that
Aristotle read the features of true deity into his First
Mover; in which case his mind will have at some time
responded to a personal divine communication, although
he had presumably misunderstood the nature of the
communication, through lack of suitable ideas by which to
interpret it.'

In turning to consider this type of position, we will fix our
attention first upon the phrase 'personal communication'.
What does it mean? On the face of it, it suggests that God
must speak to us somewhat as we speak to one another. But
this obviously does not happen, nor is it going to happen. If I
heard a divine voice in the air without, which was no appari-
tion but an actual exterior event, it would still be necessary to
suppose that the First Cause, God, was operating through
second causes, which would be physical sound-waves: for
that is exactly what I should mean by calling the voice
exterior and real. If, on the other hand, the voice is not really
exterior, but an imagination of my own mind, then the First
Cause finds his second or instrumental cause in some working
of my natural phantasy. If, again, the voice is a voice by
metaphor only, and more properly a movement of thought,
then the second cause which God employs is some part of my
mental activity; and he employs it to address in his name

6

another stream of my thinking, which is at the moment arrogating to itself the name of *me*.

Now no one, I think, who wished to make Aristotle's knowledge of God conditional upon a 'personal communication' would lay it down that he must seem to hear voices or see visions. Those would not be Aristotelian things to do, and if they are required, then all the Aristotles of this world are damned without remedy. We must take it, then, that Aristotle is to experience the address of God through the secondary causality of his own thought.

I should now like to ask how important it is deemed to be that the philosopher's experience should fall into the form of an inward colloquy, with one part of his thought addressing another as though with the voice of God. I have a special and personal interest in challenging the colloquy-form, because of an obstacle I remember encountering in my own adolescence. I had myself (this at least is the impression I retain) been reared in a personalism which might satisfy the most ardent of Dr. Buber's disciples. I thought of myself as set over against deity as one man faces another across a table, except that God was invisible and indefinitely great. And I hoped that he would signify his presence to me by way of colloquy; but neither out of the scripture I read nor in the prayers I tried to make did any mental voice address me. I believe at that time anything would have satisfied me, but nothing came: no 'other' stood beside me, no shadow of presence fell upon me. I owe my liberation from this *impasse*, as far as I can remember, to reading Spinoza's Ethics. Those phrases which now strike me as so flat and sinister, so ultimately atheistic, *Deus sive Natura* (God, or call it Nature), Deus, quatenus consideratur ut constituens essentiam humanae mentis (God, in so far as he is regarded as constituting the being of the human mind)—these phrases were to me light and liberation, not because I was or desired to be a pantheist, but because I could not find the wished-for colloquy with God.

Undoubtedly I misunderstood Spinoza, in somewhat the

same fashion as (to quote a high example) St. Augustine misunderstood Plotinus, turning him to Christian uses. Here, anyhow, is what I took from Spinozism. I would no longer attempt, with the psalmist, 'to set God before my face'. I would see him as the underlying cause of my thinking, especially of those thoughts in which I tried to think of him. I would dare to hope that sometimes my thought would become diaphanous, so that there should be some perception of the divine cause shining through the created effect, as a deep pool, settling into a clear tranquillity, permits us to see the spring in the bottom of it from which its waters rise. I would dare to hope that through a second cause the First Cause might be felt, when the second cause in question was itself a spirit, made in the image of the divine Spirit, and perpetually welling up out of his creative act.

Such things, I say, I dared to hope for, and I will not say that my hope was in any way remarkably fulfilled, but I will say that by so viewing my attempted work of prayer, I was rid of the frustration which had baffled me before. And this is why, when Germans set their eyeballs and pronounce the terrific words 'He speaks to thee' (Er redet dich an) I am sure, indeed, that they are saying something, but I am still more sure that they are not speaking to my condition.

To return now to our discussion of a most unhistorical Aristotle. What is it that the personalists demand? Must the philosopher be aware of God addressing him in mental colloquy, or will it do if he should, as St. Augustine so vividly did, perceive God as light, shining through his acts of intelligence? Or perhaps what the personalists mean is something different: that it does not matter how God touches the philosopher, whether by mental colloquy, or by shewing through his diaphanous thought, or by falling on him in the splendour of the stars; any of these ways will suffice, so long as they produce the right effect. The philosopher must be brought to realise that the God who so touches him places him in a personal relation to himself. He must acknowledge duties to the supreme worth of divine Spirit, analogous to the duties he acknowledges towards the subordinate worth of the human spirits who surround him; so that for him to say 'Thou, O God' will be no figure, as it might be in the mouth of Horace invoking the Bandusian Spring.

If this is what the personalists mean, they are no longer talking about the way in which God reveals himself to the philosopher, they are talking about the response which the revelation evokes. If Aristotle's mind is so moved by its own operation under God, and by the observed motions of the stars, that it falls into a posture of adoration, of response to an infinite person, it will then be said that God has personally revealed himself to Aristotle, and that Aristotle in consequence knows something of God. If, on the other hand, Aristotle sees God simply as ultimate being, as mainspring of cause and loadstone of motion, then it will be said that Aristotle does not know God; he knows an idol of his own mind, for God has never spoken to him.

If we have brought the matter to this point, we have brought it to an issue of verbal definition, and nothing else. In either case Aristotle, moved by the First Cause, sees things that are true of that Cause. Above all else it is true that God is the master of our life, but it is also true, so far as it goes, that he is the Self-thinking Thought on whom all finite agencies depend. Whichever thing Aristotle thinks, he has been moved by God to think truth of God. Only it is apparently proposed that the name 'God' should be given a restricted use: 'God' is to mean the Supreme Being viewed as the master of our life, personally determining us. In any other aspect he is to be called by some other name. Well, as we said before, let every man use words in such a sense as serves best to make his meaning plain; and there may be contexts in which the restricted sense proposed for the word 'God' would make for clarity. But whatever those contexts may be, anyhow the sober history of philosophical and theological thinking is not one of them.

If we were to ask, as a matter of simple fact, whether Aristotle acknowledged in God the personal master of his life, commanding a personal response on his own part, that, I fear, would happen which so often happens when we apply preconceived definitions to historical instances—we do not know whether to say that they apply, or that they do not. The astral paganism of which Aristotle's theology was so curious a refinement was no mere physical hypothesis, but a genuine, if cool and limited, spirituality. When Aristotle, crowned with evergreen, slew his victim to the highest of astral deities, and said 'Thou, O God', he did not suppose himself to be apostrophizing an abstraction or indulging an artificial personification. He was performing an act of homage towards supreme spirit, even though he would have regarded it as a derogation from that spirit's supremacy, if he should deign to hear his worshipper's words. The philosopher knew, in addition, that because God is God, and our minds bear to him some partial resemblance, therefore our highest good must be to practise the acts of godhead so far as in us lies. So much for Aristotle's creed. Whether it constitutes personal response to God, is a question we will leave to those theologians, whose position obliges them to find a *yes* or *no* answer to it.

We should ourselves like to advance, as being at least probable, the following propositions. God, working by way of nature, may lead the human mind to recognize its own supreme cause through its own proper operation. When this happens there are on the human side several degrees of consciousness possible as to what is happening. A man may suppose himself to infer God as the cause of the physical effects he studies, or as the cause of his own existence, without being aware of the divine causality behind his own act in so inferring God. Again, he may be aware of the divine causality behind his own thoughts, but as a general illumination simply, lighting up all his understanding indifferently, so far as he understands: as a candle illuminates all equidistant objects with indifferent rays. Or, finally, he may see the divine moving of his best thought as the direction of a personal providence, with which he can in a manner co-operate by attending to it. If he has reached this stage, he may be said by personalists to have responded personally to God. But it seems unreasonable, on the face of it, to deny the possibility of other and inferior degrees of consciousness in the natural knowledge of God. Surely God may lead us to the knowledge of himself without our knowing that he leads us, or without our understanding his leading in a 'personal' way. And whichever occurs of the things we have considered, there is no need to seek its explanation in a supernatural act of God: his action by way of nature could suffice.

Nevertheless there is also a supernatural action of God, or so we believe; and we must endeavour now to describe it. Let us begin by placing it in relation with the convenient distinction between the First Cause and the second causes. Not that, if God acts supernaturally, he acts without second causes; but he works through second causes effects which do not arise from the natural powers of those causes. It is by reference to the powers of second causes that events or states are called 'supernatural'. Nothing is supernatural to God, because his nature is infinity, and no action exceeds it. But many acts may be supernatural to man, because many conceivable achievements exceed his natural faculties: to learn, for example, the mystery of Trinity in the Godhead.

It must be understood in this context that by 'cause', 'agent' is meant, as should be evident from the implied comparison between First Cause and second causes. The First Cause is simply a creative agent, and not a cause in any other sense but this: not, for example, a supreme causal 'law', nor a first event upon which other events follow according to causal 'law'. The First Cause is an agent, the second causes are likewise agents or energies. If we understand 'cause' in the Kantian sense, then to talk of a cause being endowed with an efficacy beyond its natural scope, is nonsense. A Kantian may define 'cause' like this: A cause is an event belonging to a class of events, of which it is universally true that they are followed by events of a further given class. If we say that a flash of lightning is the cause of the consequent thunder, we are held to be classing the lightning as an electric explosion, and acknowledging that from all electric explosions sound-waves arise. According to this definition of 'cause', no cause can be endowed with an efficacy above what it has by nature. If an event B follows an event A otherwise than the causal law applicable to A demands, then by the Kantian definition A is not the cause of B at all, and B's cause must be sought elsewhere, in the event C, for example. We might hunt causes for B endlessly. If (to suppose an absurdity) we could establish that no cause whatever had caused B *naturally*, we could not conclude that some cause had caused it *supernaturally*, by acting, that is, beyond its natural efficacy; for we have agreed that under the Kantian definition of cause such a conclusion would not mean anything. We should simply have to say that B was apparently *uncaused*.

If we were attempting to be theists as well as Kantians (and after all, Kant attempted it) we might (though Kant would not) attach the event B direct to the causality of God; we might say that it had no second cause, but was an immediate new creation of the First. Such a conclusion may seem at first sight delightful to the pious mind; but a little reflection will shew us that the piety which delights in it must be of the sort to believe the absurd for its own sake. For if we attach the supernatural event simply to the First Cause alone, it is then no part of the existing finite world, having no real connexion with the sequence of finite occurrences: it is a fragment of a new world momentarily interpolated into the old. But that is not (I hope) what we mean by the supernatural. When the supernatural occurs, something in the existing world is supernaturalized, for example, the manhood of Jesus Christ by union with the deity, or, to take a legendary instance, Balaam's ass by being enabled to speak.

The story of Balaam is highly instructive for our purpose.

It represents the point at which the magic supernatural comes under divine control. We can easily reconstruct an older Balaam, a figure of pure fairy tale. He is the mighty magician, whose spells are efficacious of themselves. He rides an ass which, in the crisis of her master's destiny—when he is about to collide with an invisible armed magician of power greater than his own—of herself opens her mouth and speaks. Such may have been the original story: but as we have it, it has become something different. Balaam's power of efficacious spell is a supernatural gift from God, and woe betide him if he attempts to use it otherwise than the divine will allows. His ass is no more than an ass, until God gives her a power beyond her asinine nature, that she may be able to warn her master from fighting against God.

I hope it will cause no scandal if I simply confess that the theologizing of the magical represents the historical beginning of the supernatural, as we have to define it. In the fairy-tale world it is simply accepted that things and persons act from time to time beyond their determinate 'natures'. The fairy-tale takes the world to consist of real active beings which act of themselves—and this at least is as good philosophy as it is good faery. The real active beings of fairy-land are of various determinate kinds: men, women, dogs, asses, trees, stones. These beings normally act within the rule of their natural kind, for that is what is meant by saying that they belong to such a kind. On occasion, however, they exert a higher efficacy, developing, as it were, a supernatural margin to the line of their natural act: men ride the wind, asses speak, and rocks obey the human voice. We reach the end of fairy-land and pass the boundary-stone which the Balaam-story represents, and such wonders are still said to befall, but only through the supernaturalizing of natural agents by God.

I said that I hoped the confession of such lowly beginnings for supernaturalism would cause no offence. I will try now to explain why it need not. I will do this by raising the question, how it is initially possible for the human mind to conceive supernatural action at all. I reply that the possibility derives from the very form of our active existence. We are primarily aware of ourselves as active beings, engaged in interaction with a whole environment of other active beings. We are further aware that we can, of ourselves, vary the form of our activity, from working to eating, from digging to planting. We are also aware that we can, to an astonishing degree, vary the intensity of our activity, from lounging to running for our lives, from day-dreaming to hard thinking. We can also vary the elevation of our act, from eating food like a beast to shaping verse like an angel. All our alternative acts are controlled by the subtle and expansible pattern of our human nature. But within that pattern we have large scope of freedom, and the sense of such freedom easily begets the dream of passing right beyond our nature into supernatural action. What we dream for ourselves, we attribute to others, to dogs, asses, trees and stones, and the world of faery appears.

Yet the idea of unaided supernatural action on the part of any agent is, on the face of it, almost a contradiction in terms; even in the fairy world there is a tendency to attribute the supernatural efficacy of a natural agent to the aid of other beings: beings not necessarily superior in all respects to the agent, but possessing anyhow by nature the type of active power which they are supposed to confer upon him. We say that unaided supernatural action is almost a contradiction in terms. For the 'nature' of an active being, by definition, determines the scope of his unaided action: if *of himself* he acted beyond what he and we supposed his nature to be, we ought to conclude forthwith that we had defined his nature too narrowly, not that he had exceeded it.

The idea of the supernatural is of a finite agent exceeding his natural power by higher assistance. The idea is common to religious thought at many levels: rank superstition, primitive barbarism and high spirituality will all make their own applications of it, for all are concerned with the elevation of man to what lies above him. For us, the typical case of the supernatural is not seen in physical miracles, but in the empowering of the spirit of man by the Spirit of his Creator, to know and to love the supreme and causeless Act, the pure and endless Being, the saving Charity: *to whom therefore, one God in three Persons, Father, Son and Holy Ghost, be ascribed, as is most justly due, all might, dominion, majesty and power, henceforth and for ever.*

II

O give thanks unto the Lord, for he is gracious; for his mercy endureth for ever. Who alone doeth great wonders; for his mercy endureth for ever. PSALM CXXXVI, 1-4

Our purpose here is further to examine the idea of a super-natural act in the human mind, when it knows God by way of revelation.

In the last fifty years the discussion of the supernatural has changed its character. The old critics of the supernatural, the physical dogmatists, thought they knew pretty nearly the bounds of nature, and stubbornly disbelieved anything which appeared to pass them. The new critics of the supernatural are, on the contrary, only too ready to believe in the occurrence of wonders. What they deny is that the bounds of nature can be fixed at all. Nature is so various and so queer, they think, that what were once thought miracles may be perfectly natural occurrences.

We note this particularly in the discussion of uncanny forms of psychical action by our psychical researchers. These people of course admit a rough distinction between the normal and the abnormal in our experience. But those of them who have the best claim to be thought scientific use the axiom that the abnormal is still the action of finite agents, and though not normal, natural. To take the example of telepathy. If a sailor drowning at sea makes an impress on the mind of his wife in harbour, he is held to be exerting a power which belongs to human nature as such, and is available for exercise under conditions ideally capable of definition, however difficult it may be in practice to define them. The song which the psychical researchers sing in our ears is this, that human nature, and

16

the natures of the forces which compose human environment, are other than we had supposed, and infinitely more complex.

It is reasonable to agree with the psychical researchers, so far as the phenomena go which they investigate. But if so, have we any room left to assert the supernatural at all? How, we must ask ourselves, could the genuine supernatural ever be evidenced? How can we ever be sure that any exerted act is beyond the nature of the agent exerting it, if the nature of the agent is so difficult to fix? Must not we conclude that the idea of the supernatural is simply an illusion? Especially since it is so easy to see how the illusion should arise. It is almost inevitable, is it not, that men should misconceive their natural limits, drawing them too narrowly, and ruling out the abnormal. The abnormal occurs, and we falsely suppose that our active power has run beyond the limits of our nature. Such is the first step on the road to superstition. The second quickly follows: we refer our supposed supernatural act to divine influences acting upon us. For since no agent can exert a power he has not got, we look about for some magical agent outside us who has bestowed on us for the occasion the excess power of which we dispose.

The reference of supposedly supernatural acts to a supernaturalizing influence from without comes all the more readily, because in many abnormal activities we have the feeling of possession or alien control. His best verses are 'given' to the poet; the fortune-teller cannot predict by a direct volition, but by somehow making his mind expectantly passive, and waiting for images to delineate themselves; and so on. A psychologist will have no difficulty in explaining the appearance of alien control in such cases. It is well-known that there are functions of our mind, and indeed of our bodies, which are not controlled by direct will-power, but can sometimes be induced, as it were, to act by ancillary volitions releasing them. Since we identify ourselves with the releasing volitions by the mere fact of making them, we are liable to experience as other than ourselves the action of the functions they release. There is no special mystery about this to a psychologist, but our ancestors were not psychologists, and the phenomenon of apparent alien control must powerfully have helped them to ascribe supposedly supernatural acts to mysterious influences whereby they were enabled to operate.

Such considerations as those we have been entertaining must force a theologian to subject the traditional doctrine of the supernatural to a searching criticism. A test case, for example, will be the healing miracles of Christ. An older and simpler age dogmatically pronounced: as man he hungered and thirsted, as God he healed the lame and blind. In view of the facts of psychological healing now known to us, many of us feel doubt about placing the healing simply upon the divine side. Ought we not to say that powers of psychological healing belonged to Christ's human nature as such? Believers will wish to add that, like other of his human powers, they were enhanced by the taking of Christ's nature into the deity of God the Son: they were, in fact, supernaturally enhanced. But 'enhanced' is not 'conferred': what is now said to be supernatural is not the appearance of such powers, but the degree in which they appear. So a believer may say. An unbeliever, it is obvious, will view this as a position taken up overnight in the course of a theological rearguard action, and not destined to be defended either successfully or for long. We are in full retreat, he will think, towards a wholly non-supernatural religion.

We do not, in fact, view our own predicament with any serious solicitude, nor are we preparing to throw supernaturalism overboard. Let us recur to the definition of supernatural action. It is action which is *above* what our nature allows of. Now psychical research may have left us less clear than we were as to the sideways and downward limits of our natural powers; but it has done nothing, so far as I can see, to raise or unfix the ceiling. We can still speak with confidence about the supernatural, because we know just as much as we did before about the upward limit of our powers. About the *preternatural* as a whole we cannot speak with the same confidence, not being able to fix our limit so clearly in other directions.

The distinction just drawn between the preternatural in general and the more specially supernatural is vital to our argument. It is bound, I am afraid, to land us in considerable complexities of exposition. They will have to be endured, for if we shirk them we shall be unable to say anything of use. To begin with, we shall be called upon to justify the antithesis between an upward limit and a sideways and downwards limit to our faculties. Are any acts we perform intrinsically 'higher' than any others? Do not we call an ability 'high' simply because we are in fact reaching after it with effort, like a man picking fruit from a tall tree? Are not all abilities 'high' in this sense, provided they lie at or beyond the furthest stretch of our powers? Fortune-tellers stretch to obtain premonitions of the future, and mystics to obtain union with their Creator, and scientists to formulate an adequate hypothesis, and statesmen to devise the prevention of public ruin. All these aims are in themselves good or innocent, and all of them are on the tips of the branches. Is one intrinsically 'higher' than another?

We are bound to reply that there is, in fact, a hierarchy of human acts, some higher, or nobler, in themselves than others; this is a first metaphysical truth. If acts were 'high' in proportion to their difficulty, then the gymnastic feat of picking that last apple 'which furthest blushes on the furthest bough' without breaking either the tree or one's own neck—a feat, let us suppose, of fantastic muscular virtuosity—might be as 'high' as the act of finding a fresh solution to a main philosophical problem. It is no use replying, 'Ah, but the apple-picking is a bodily feat,' for we do not solve philosophical problems without the instrumentality of our nerves; any more than (conversely) we pick the apple without judgment and

19

resolution. As the action of a frog is a higher form of action than the action of a cog, and the action of a dog than that of a frog: so is human action higher than canine action, and, within the human field, those acts which are more specially human, than those which are nearer to the animal level; and chimpanzees can pick awkwardly placed apples with greater skill than we can.

There is a hierarchy in the order of human acts: we all know this well enough in principle, however hard we may find it to determine the hierarchical grade of a given act. We will assume the principle of hierarchy without more ado, and proceed to relate it to the knowledge of our own upward limit. For we have said that we know our upward limit more clearly than we do our sideways and downward limit. The truth which we hope to make plain is that the knowledge of our upward limit is equivalent to our self-knowledge, for, in a sense, we do know ourselves.

Psychical researchers may try to make our flesh creep by telling us that our conventional idea of our personal being has little if any relation to the truth; that our mind, instead of being limited in space to the operation of our nervous system, and in time to the present moment, and in scope to our conscious acts, is prowling all over the place on its own, ranging into the past and future, and the merest fraction of it deigning to appear in consciousness at all. And the psycho-analysts, with their investigations into the plumbing and the cellarage of our volitional life, may seem to give us much the same impression: the self we know is a mere surface phenomenon floating on an unsounded deep. Yet even if we grant all the particular facts asserted by the psychologists and psychic researchers to be true, we still feel an instinctive suspicion that the negative conclusion drawn with respect to our self-knowledge belongs to rhetoric and not to science.

One of the things which makes us suspicious is that we have heard all this before, in a closely parallel field. As psychic researchers may tell us that we do not know our own souls, so physicists and physiologists may tell us that we do not know our own bodily being. Are not the vital processes of our anatomy complex beyond anything that lay common-sense supposes? And do not those processes organize an infinity of cells, of whose distinct existence we never had the least notion? And does not each cell, in turn, organize an infinity of physical atoms? And has not each atom within it a system of forces of the sort, which, artificially released in sufficient quantity, blew a Japanese city to pieces the other day? Need we go further? Is it not plain that our bodies are each a universe in itself, of which our ordinary bodily consciousness gives us no least idea?

Even under the beating of so many waves of interrogative rhetoric we should none of us, I take it, have much difficulty in keeping our feet. We should readily reply: All this is irrelevant. What I mean by my body is the system of physical motion and sensation in which I live: that is why I call it mine, and why I regard it as a unit. In direct consciousness of having, or being, or using my body, I have an inward understanding of what bodily life is, of what it is to be embodied and alive, which nothing else but simple and direct consciousness can possibly give: anatomy adds nothing to it. I am aware, of course, that the experienced and living form of the body itself uses, permeates, indwells a certain amount of stuff. To speak more exactly of the body, I mean by it the felt pattern of animal life, taken not in abstraction, but together with so much stuff as it directly controls, permeates and depends upon. But in defining the body I do not define the nature of that stuff, I merely state that there is a good deal of it. In the same way, if I were defining a chair, I should assume that it was made of some suitable material, but I should not include oak or mahogany or steel-tubing in my definition. I already know what a chair is before I lift the petticoat of chintz to see what the feet are made of, and I already know what my body is before I begin anatomy or biology or physics. These sciences will tell me a great deal about the

subsidiary forms which the form of the living body orga-
nizes; and in so doing they will tell me a great deal about the
conditions which determine the functioning of the bodily
form, or even make it possible for the bodily form to function at all. But what I mean by 'human body' is simply the
bodily form itself, thought of as organizing whatever subsidiary forms it does organize: and the special sciences cast no
direct light on what it is to be that bodily form. It is lit up by
one thing, and one thing alone—the embodied consciousness
of the man whose body is in question. The problem of bodily
knowledge is, as we see, solved immediately by the principle
of hierarchy. We define the body by its highest organizing
principle, and, because that remains unaltered, the body continues to answer to the same definition, whatever may be
revealed about the subsidiary organisms within it. Even
though it turns out to consist of a virtual infinity of distinct
real parts, and even though each one of these parts stands in
real causal relation with every other element of matter in the
whole universe, our body remains, in virtue of its highest
form, just what we perceive it to be. We might use the figure
of a cone to illustrate the point. If we are looking at a cone
whose apex alone is in clear light, we can determine what
sort of a cone it is, even though we do not know how far
downwards and outwards its base extends into the dark.

To turn now from the body to the mind. The mind likewise is known for what it is by the highest principle in its
hierarchic constitution, not by the indefinite multitude of
subsidiary elements: by the luminous apex, not by the spread-
ing shadowy base. Mind is known in rational consciousness,
where intelligence reflects upon itself, and choice designs the
act it initiates. We do not mean by the mind simply this
luminous apex, we are dimly aware besides of an obscure
psychic mass on which it feeds: all the materials which
remain in memory when we are not remembering, all the
directions of desire and interest which go on pointing, when
we are neither desiring nor interesting ourselves in their aims:

and so on. But we should know nothing of all this obscure psychic stuff, if it did not affect consciousness itself from time to time, or if consciousness did not presuppose it: or anyhow we should not regard the shadowy base as any part of the *mind*, unless we perceived that the luminous apex fed upon it.

Now in so far as philosophers or psychologists are really describing the luminous apex of our human spirit, all they can do is to draw to a greater precision what we already know ourselves to be, and if we do not recognise the portrait, we shall rightly reject it. If they want to make our flesh creep or our mouths gape, they must tell us about the shadowy base of the mind, where special techniques and special observations enable them plausibly to establish a great deal about us which never entered into our waking thoughts. But this does not mean that our whole self-knowledge becomes unfixed, for self-knowledge is not a sort of wide statistical generalization based equally on all the facts discoverable about any and every region of our mind. Self-knowledge has a hierarchical structure: it is the knowledge of the luminous apex of consciousness, taken as supported by such a psychic base as it may be found to have.

Let us now recall the thesis which led us into all this somewhat ambitious effort after philosophical definition. We were saying, were we not, that a serious and a determinate sense can be given to the supernatural, because our human nature has a sharply defined top or apex, so that anything above it must be supernatural to us: whereas we were prepared to admit that the sideways and downwards limits of our nature are all unfixed, so that it is hard for us to feel any confidence that any of the apparently preternatural is really preternatural and not merely abnormal, apart from the truly *super* natural. What we now hope is that the doctrine of the cone may do something to justify confidence in the fixity of our human apex, however indeterminate our lower fringes may be. But we cannot hope to get away with the argument so lightly. We shall be told that however convincing the doctrine of the cone may appear by the light of pure reason, it will not stand up to empirical fact. The doctrine of the cone suggests that our highest act is our centrally human act, by which we define ourselves; and that the obscure and hair-raising matter brought before us by psychical researchers is all related to the lower and subordinate levels of the soul. But this, it may be objected, is simply not true. In obscure abnormal actions which appear to be neither voluntary nor intelligent in the common sense, the human mind performs some of its most godlike feats. By a sort of alienation of consciousness the seer escapes from the bonds of space and time and ranges into the future or to the other side of the planet. And, by unaccountable processes which are certainly not under direct rational control, the poet's mind throws up the golden line to be the corner-stone of the lyric, and the physicist's mind projects the new master-hypothesis. How then can it be maintained that the psychically odd belongs to the bottom of the soul?

We must, in reply, distinguish here. We cannot allow the weird phenomena of clairvoyance, clairaudience, telepathy and prediction to be tied up in one bundle with the noble achievements of inspiration. We must have two bundles and take them separately. Let us take the noble inspirations first. We entirely agree that they belong to the top of the soul, for they are nothing but the specially striking manifestations of a power which accompanies rational consciousness throughout. The excellence of the mind consists of conscious intelligence, but of a conscious intelligence based always upon acute senses and riding upon a vigorous imagination. For although the excellence of the mind is the act of thinking, the act of thinking is not self-sufficient, but has constant recourse to the imagination; and out of such recourse wit and (in the secular sense) inspiration arise. But what springs up though wit and inspiration is not the gratuitous gift of the imagination to the intelligence: the previous labour of the intelligence is thrown down into the imagination as into a cauldron, from which it emerges again fused into new figures and, it may be, enriched with materials from the subconscious sphere, which were never in distinct consciousness at all. Newton's hypothesis and Shakespeare's tragedy were the product of acute and lively intelligence exercised in the appropriate fields. The moments of inspiration may have been apparently passive, even compulsive and as it were invasive: but they would not have occurred but for previous intellectual labour, nor would they have been of any significance if they had not been seized and elaborated by the same intellectual power which had been their remoter cause. In inspired wit a spark leaps from intelligence to intelligence across a field of imagination: whereas in weird abnormal consciousness the spark leaps from the outer dark into imagination itself, providing an image of which the intelligence must make what it can. Inspired wit is a normal part of the life of the minds' conscious apex: without some measure of it we can do nothing but work out sums and syllogisms according to pre-established rules from pre-established premises. It is vain to ask whether wit or reason is the apex of the mind, for neither exists without the other. When inspiration closely accompanies intelligence, we are unaware of it as a distinct power. But when it has a great work to do, it sometimes specializes itself: there is a sort of gap in the intellectual process, a relaxation and suppling of the mind, a throwing of the reins on the horse's neck: presently inspiration strikes into its new path, and intelligence resumes control. Such experiences amaze us, but there is nothing abnormal about them in kind: it is simply a matter of degree. The apex of the mind remains what it supposes itself to be, in spite of the rare experiences of higher inspiration: for the mind does not, in fact, suppose itself to be devoid of wit at any time.

So, then, of the two bundles of mysterious phenomena which are alleged to extend our mental scope above the top of the mind, the one bundle, that of noble inspiration, belongs to what has always been recognized as making up the top of the mind itself, wit and reason. Such inspiration (always using the word in the secular sense) belongs to what is most godlike in the natural man: but it also belongs to what is most centrally human in him. Now to take the other bundle of mysterious phenomena, the weird events that are the special subject of psychical research. They really do fall outside what we commonly take to be human nature: but they are not godlike in the least; they belong to the bottom of the mind. Clairvoyance, clairaudience and foresight would be godlike if such powers were either controllable in their exercise, or determinate and unambiguous in their discoveries: but they are not. It would be godlike if the psychically gifted man could send his mind on a mission, whenever he chose, as Prospero sent Ariel, to sight what was happening to a given person at a given place or time, and return him instantaneously a clear report. It cannot be done. The most the gifted person can do is to let his divinatory power loose, as it were, in connexion with a given person or in the area of a given subject of interest, and see what images it brings back. The images, if they come, carry no guarantee of relevance or genuineness, seldom any clear marks of place, date or circumstance, and, worst of all, no certain rule for their own interpretation. Spinoza coined a phrase for his own use which will exactly fit ours—'loose experience', *experientia vaga*. For if anything deserves the name, it is the weird experience which we are discussing. It is plausible to suppose that primitive consciousness had it in far greater degree than our more advanced consciousness has it. As though the mind had begun with a small centre of clear intelligence, and a wide penumbra of vague sensitivity to environment, to the near and the distant, the past, present and future, all unplaced, uninterpreted, confused; and that mentality as we know it has been achieved by the suppression of all this *experientia vaga* through the expansion of practical, controlled and determinate intellect, kept workable by close restriction to the present moment and the five senses. The weird experience which we come across in our own day may be more like a primitive survival than a foretaste of higher development. Even so, our whole power to make anything of the weird data depends on our firm grasp of the everyday world through precise, time-bound and sensebound experience. Normal consciousness supplies us with our mental map of the world, and it is on this map that we place, if we can place, the data of *experientia vaga*. Nobody could make anything at all of a whole world of *experientia vaga* and nothing else: it would be a kaleidoscope of shifting dreams. Only the luminous apex of the mind can do anything with it. *Experientia vaga* belongs to the bottom of the soul.

To say that the psychically weird belongs to the bottom of the soul is not of course to deny that it may be made the instrument of noble acts and purposes. After all, what most of the weird phenomena amount to is roughly this, that whereas we used to think that our minds touched the rest of the world through our own bodies alone, we may now have to admit that they touch it at many other points besides: and especially that our minds touch one another without bodily intervention. If this is a fact, it is just a fact about the way in which the multitude of finite things jostle one another in one universe. As there is nothing specially godlike in the fact that our bodies touch, so there is nothing specially godlike in the fact (if it is a fact) of our spirits touching. Physical contact is nothing godlike, and yet through physical contact a compassionate will can perform those acts which will redeem it from everlasting fire and set it on the right hand of the divine Shepherd—to feed the hungry, to clothe the naked and to visit the captive. So psychical contact will be merely contact, yet of what may not it be made the instrument? Christians believe that their acts of prayer may, under God, assist their neighbours' souls, and it seems likely that the touch of mind on mind has something to do with that. Christians believe also that the charity of departed saints can assist us in this world, and our prayers assist the departed in their purgation:

there is an interchange of spiritual act among the members of Christ's body, as though all, in some way, touched one another. There is certainly something godlike here, but it is not the touching, it is what the touching is made to convey—supernatural charity. The exercise of the praying act is god-like, not the contact by which it affects (if it does so affect) another's mind: that is mere mechanics, and might be the vehicle of bad influence as well as good. We pray with the apex of the mind, with the intelligent will, with what we have always known to be the very principle of our selfhood. And if, in praying, we reach above that apex into what, transcending our nature, is supernatural to us, it is not in touching our neighbours, it is in touching God.

In a sense, no doubt, we touch him by the very fact of our existence, for does not it momently spring out of his creative act? Such a contact, if it is to be called a contact, is not supernatural to us, for it belongs to our nature to be continually created. But if we can rise out of our dependent selves and penetrate the mind of him on whom we depend, then we climb above the top of ourselves and achieve a supernatural act.

Let us consider a little more carefully how far the natural knowledge of God extends, and where the supernatural will begin. I must as a Christian believe that my existence is throughout a two-sided fact. On the one side it is the active being of a second cause, myself, in dependence upon, and interaction with, other second causes. On the other side it is the continual effect of the first cause, God. The total fact is never myself alone, not even myself with the world for its environment, but always my world-environed self, *and God*. My existence has these two active centres always. Not that they can be for a moment placed in equipoise. The centre called 'I' is not a centre at all when considered in relation to God, but more properly a point on the circumference of his action. An impartial view of the double fact of myself and God would simply be God's view, identified with him, operating from his centre. God's view is the view of mind as such, for it corresponds to the real structure of existence. The tendency of any mind, in proportion as it overcomes its creaturely limitations, must be to gravitate towards the divine centre, and share the divine view of things. That is the goal; it cannot be the starting point. So as to be a creaturely mind, a being distinct from God, I must be, and am, the mind of a creaturely centre, closely identified with the operation of a second cause, and viewing things either as they condition that cause, or as it can condition them.

My knowledge is the knowledge of my own active existence. Yet the limitation of my knowledge to the field of my own finitude does not involve me in the supreme lie about it, the supposition that it is *uncaused*. On the contrary: the natural mind may know of God whatever is involved in the perception of its own necessary dependence upon him, as of secondary upon primary being and act. What the finite mind perceives in detail and fullness is always finite existence: what it perceives of God is the bare form of an absolute act, seen as enacting the various multiplicity of finite existence.

Now such knowledge might, in an ideal case, amount to a great deal. If we reconstruct the legendary unfallen Adam, if we give him the intellect of Aristotle, the natural spirituality of St. Paul without the gifts of revelation, and the charitable humility of St. Francis unenhanced by supernatural faith, we may imagine in such a mind the perfection of mere theism, mere creator-worship. His awareness of God need not be limited to the knowledge of abstract propositions about him and his agency; the divine agency might be read in the creaturely effects, external nature and his own existence might be experienced as the continual work of God. Especially his own highest acts and desires might be acknowledged as having a source in himself only in so far as he was himself grounded in God. He might practise continual prayer by the continual aspiration to draw the life of his spirit up from the well of infinity, or rather, to open the channels of his mind to be irrigated from that unfailing spring. He might see in God's direction a providence, tending towards the perfection of the natural in all its forms, a fostering charity towards all creatures. This would be much, but none of it need be supernatural, for it would not exceed the perception of God's agency, simply in so far as nature and natural perfections express it. It would interpret God by two things alone: by the created world, and by the general bare idea of first agent cause. Its subjective instruments would be the intelligence and wit of the mind's natural apex, employed upon their natural object, finite existence.

If all this can be natural knowledge (though so much, perhaps, never occurs except by way of accompaniment to knowledge supernaturally given), what knowledge would be distinctively supernatural? Any knowledge would be so, which transposed us, as it were, to the divine centre of activity: which gave us to know, not the bare idea of such a centre, but anything about the way in which the life there lived is exercised and enjoyed at its own divine level: anything which reveals to us the activity of God in God. But it is equally possible to conceive supernatural knowledge about God's activity in the world. Suppose, for example, that God is fulfilling purposes in his direction of finite beings, which are not manifested in the present action and existence of those beings. From the fact that the craftsman is preparing materials you may guess that he is about some work, but it may be impossible for men or angels to infer what the work is to be, without communication with the craftsman's mind: and God's conduct of the universe may be of that sort. Only by shifting our centre from ourselves to him, by communion with his mind, could we know the work of God through nature, in so far as it transcends the purposes of nature as nature; or rather, of nature as what we can apprehend nature to be.

To proceed to examples: the Christian faith claims to possess supernatural truth in both the fields that we have specified. It tells of the life of God in God, and it tells of divine purposes in the natural world transcending nature. It says that in God there is an act of begotten and responsive love, that it is reciprocated, and that it is cemented by a Spirit mutually indwelling. And it says that in the created world there is a work of salvation, whereby mortal spirits are supernaturalized, and drawn into the participation of eternal being. You may think if you will that these mysterious truths are no truths at all: but if they are truths, they are not, in the human mind, natural truths: they are not, that is to say, the fruit of natural human acts, for by no such act could we be reasonably assured of their genuineness. For the life of God in its divine centre is not given me, by nature, to reflect upon. I am not there with him, I am here with myself.

But who exercises the supernatural act by which supernatural truths are known? If you and I suppose we know such things by faith, is the supernatural apprehension ours, or can we borrow the supernatural truths from the supernatural apprehension of an inspired mediator, without ourselves exercising any supernatural act? Let us begin to answer this question by a fictitious simplification. Let us allow ourselves to talk about 'man' set over against God. We shall then have to say that, if any supernatural truth is ever to be known by 'man', God must make 'man' to perform a supernatural act in apprehending God's self-communication. But when we proceed to split up this fictitious subject 'man' into the multitude of believers in one supernatural faith, the distribution of supernatural activity amongst them will not be equal. To Christ's manhood belongs unique supernaturality of act, to the apostles and evangelists their proper grade, and to the saints a higher degree than to us. Yet in our degree we all participate in supernatural act, for we do not receive revealed truth as simply a tale told about God in the third person by others; we apprehend it as assured to us by God himself, or to put it otherwise, the description of divine mysteries ceases to be experienced by us as mere description: in the lines laid down by the description, the mysteries shine with their own light and presence; or rather, with the light and presence of God. Here there is a *guided* supernatural apprehension on our part, but a supernatural apprehension nevertheless. If a child cannot walk unsupported, that is not to say that he is simply dragged, and does not walk at all.

There is a sort of paradox involved in the very idea of a supernatural act. It must be the act of the natural agent, and, to be his, it must surely be absolutely continuous with his natural activity, for it is in virtue of his natural activity that he is himself. If the supernatural act were discontinuous with his natural action, it would be something that happened to him, or in connexion with him, rather than something which he did. On the other hand, if it is absolutely continuous with his natural activity, will not it of necessity be natural itself? This paradox certainly provokes deep reflection: and I must confess that, in the case of such alleged supernatural acts as that of Balaam's ass in addressing the prophet, the paradox defeats me. In what sense can it be said that asinine life, supernaturally enhanced, runs out into the utterance of good articulate speech without, as it were, getting cut off from its natural base, and falling completely out of the subjective unity of asinine action?

The apparent absurdity in the case of the ass is due to the fact that one sort of finite nature is credited with an act distinctive of another sort of finite nature; the ass behaves like a man in a point of behaviour at which the asinine excludes the human. The finite excludes another finite of incompatible nature. But in the serious case of the supernatural, which is at the heart of our religion, we are not concerned with the attribution to man of an act proper to some other finite kind, say to a grade of the angelic hierarchy: we are concerned with the opening of the finite to the infinite. Now it is by no means clear that the finite excludes the infinite in the sense in which one finite excludes another. Every mystery of religion, indeed one may say the very possibility of any spiritual religion, presupposes that it does not. I am enacting my life, you are enacting yours: I cannot enact yours nor you mine. But in some true sense the creature and the Creator are both enacting the creature's life, though in different ways and at different depths: in the second cause the first cause operates. Upon this double personal agency in our one activity turns the verbally insoluble riddle of grace and freewill, or of Godhead and Manhood in Christ's One Person, or of the efficacy of human prayer; indeed there is no issue theologians discuss which is not conditioned by it. There is no question then of the finite excluding the infinite, as the finite excludes the finite. We can, no doubt, state the limiting case: there is a point beyond which infinite God could not divinize his creature without removing its distinct creaturely nature, and as it were merging it in himself: an act which would be exactly equivalent to its annihilation. But, short of this, we can set no limits to the supernatural enhancement God can bestow. He who has by a first act created us, harmoniously extends our operation by a second. There is nothing non-human in what we are thus enabled to do: it is not the act of some other creature tacked on to us; it is simply the act of man enabled to receive divine communication, and not the act of any other sort of being in the world.

Thus, in exercising such an act, we are aware of going into a new dimension, but we are aware of no discontinuity. The act of supernatural faith appears to be only a fresh elevation of the faith we put in other things not brutally evident to sense, for example, our own moral seriousness or other men's genuine care for us. The mysteries of faith must fit into one universe of sense with our natural knowledge of human personality, of history, of the form of nature, of the first principles of being: if they did not, they would not continue to be believed. The judgment upon which faith is based is an *aestimatio* like that used in other fields. Faith leaps beyond it, but that happens too in common life; our faith in the good-will of a friend goes beyond and leaves behind any weighing of the evidence for it, and becomes a rooted axiom of living. In the case of the friend, such an axiom may be rooted, but not be ineradicable: our friend may disappoint us. As the prophet says, the mother may forget her sucking child; but God will not forget Jerusalem.

Now therefore to the one unchanging God, the Father, Son and Holy Ghost, be ascribed as is most justly due all might, dominion, majesty and power, henceforth and for ever.

III

In the preceding lectures we have considered the mere idea of supernatural action in the mind, and especially in its knowledge of God. Such knowledge bestows an apprehension of divine mysteries, inaccessible to natural reason, reflection, intuition or wit. Christians suppose such mysteries to be communicated to them through the scriptures. In particular, we believe that in the New Testament we can as it were overhear men doing supernatural thinking of a privileged order, with pens in their hands. I wish to make a fresh examination of this phenomenon. For I am not content simply to believe that supernatural thinking takes place, nor simply to accept and contemplate what it reveals, according to my own capacity. I desire to know something more in particular about the form and nature of that supernatural thinking. I may be told that it is sectarian of me to limit my study to the Christian Scriptures. But a man must limit his study to something, and it is as well to talk about what one knows, and what one, in fact, thinks most important. I speak of the Christian Revelation as Revelation *par excellence*, as Revelation simply and without qualification, for such I believe it to be. The degree in which other faiths have something of revelation in them, and the manner in which they are related to Christ's revelation, are matters which I well know to be worthy of discussion, but I beg leave not to discuss them.

No doubt the inspiration of the Scriptures will seem to many people a topic so old and so wearisome that it can be no longer endured. But if so, it will either be because they have no interest in the Scriptures themselves, or because they have not discovered what the Scriptures are good for. Anyone who has felt, even in the least degree, the power of these texts to enliven the soul and to open the gates of heaven must have some curiosity about the manner in which the miracle is worked. And, looking about him, he will quickly realize that interests more vital than those of curiosity are at stake. The prevalent doctrine about Scriptural inspiration largely determines the use men make of the Scriptures. When verbal inspiration was held, men nourished their souls on the Scriptures, and knew that they were fed. Liberal enlightenment claims to have opened the scriptural casket, but there appears now to be nothing inside—nothing, anyhow, which ordinary people feel moved to seek through the forbidding discipline of spiritual reading.

In taking up the topic of Scriptural inspiration, we should like to attach ourselves to the thought of the ancient Church: but this, we are told, is just what we have not to do. For, it is said, pre-modern thought on the subject was vitiated by a single and cardinal false assumption—the assumption that revelation was given in the form of propositions. The sacred writers were supposed to have been moved by it matters not what process of mind to put down on paper a body of propositions which, as they stand on the paper, are *de facto* inerrant. These propositions, interpreted by the light of one another and apprehended through the Church's supernatural faith, gave an account of the saving mysteries as perfect as the condition of earthly man allowed him to receive.

This being the assumption, the question of inspiration could be opened up in two directions. Either one might ask, what sort of control was exercised by the Divine Spirit over the writer, to get the propositions safely down on to the page. Or one might take up the propositions themselves, and ask in what sense they truly signified supernatural realities—whether literally or spiritually; whether univocally or analogically.

It is now impossible, we are told, to get anywhere from here. We now recognize that the propositions on the Scriptural page express the response of human witnesses to divine events, not a miraculous divine dictation. The ancient theory, it might appear, gave a senselessly duplicated account of revelation. The primary revelation, on any showing, was Christ, His life, words, passion, resurrection; and Providence was careful to provide fit witnesses of these events. But now, it appears, the occurrence of the events in the presence of the witnesses is of no practical importance, nor are they allowed to report according to their natural abilities: a few of them are seized by the Spirit, to be made the instruments of a supernatural dictation; and that is what the world will read for ever. It is as though a number of shorthand writers had been solemnly engaged to take down a supposedly extempore oration, and then the orator's secretary were to come round after its delivery and say that as a matter of fact he had got a complete text of the speech in manuscript, and would dictate it to them slowly, so that they could write it in long hand: for his employer had no faith in them, and was convinced from previous experience that they would have jumbled their notes.

Revolting from such absurdities, we say that the revelation was the fulfilment of the divine events in the presence of sufficient witnesses: as for the scripture, it is just the record of the witnesses', or their successors', reaction to the events. It is what St. Luke couldn't help fancying someone's having said he thought he remembered St. Peter's having told him: or it is the way St. Paul felt about what Christ meant to him. As for the terms in which St. Paul expressed it—well, there you are—he used any sort of figure that came to hand: he picked up a rhetorical metaphor from a cynic preaching in the market; he turned a commonplace of the synagogue pulpit inside out. He would have been amazed to learn that subsequent generations would make such stuff the foundation of dogmas. We should strip off the fashions of speech; but keep the substance, of course. But what is the substance? It has an uncanny trick of evaporating once its accidents of expression are all removed. Still, let us not acknowledge defeat. At the very least we can safely conclude that Christ had for St. Paul a supremely high numinous and ethical value; that he inspired him with new ideals, curing his bad habits, inhibitions and worries. What more does a Christian need to know? Let the modern believer nourish his soul on that. Yes: but to do it, does he really need to read St. Paul? He usually thinks not, and it is difficult to refute him.

It does not seem as though the theory of revelation by divine events alone is any more satisfactory than the theory of dictated propositions. At a pinch it will suffice for an account of the historical aspect of Scripture. The events occurred, and we get some sort of usually second-hand report about them with which we must make do. But what did the events mean? It is about this that St. Paul and St. John have been taken as inspired authorities. The theory we are considering makes them authorities for no more than the way they and their contemporaries were feeling about what God had done. It denies that they were inspired at all, in the technical sense. No doubt they had the Spirit, but then, have not we all? They were inspired as St. Francis or St. Bernard or John Wesley was inspired. The New Testament is not *uniquely* inspired (though some of its pages may be supreme in this kind). It is, however, uniquely informative, because through it the divine events, and their impact on their age, are made known to us. No other writings can replace it as the channel through which the revealing events come to us.

It does not seem good enough to say that the Scriptures are uniquely informative, but not uniquely inspired, for two reasons. It gives us bare historical events, which by themselves simply are not the Christian revelation, and says they are our only revelation; denying authority to the apostolic interpretation of the events which alone can make them a revelation. And it denies to the text of St. Paul and St. John the super-

38

naturally revealing character which Christian experience has constantly found in it.

Let us now attempt to construct some account of scriptural inspiration from first principles. This at least in modern thought upon the subject is true: the primary revelation is Jesus Christ himself. When we were talking previously about supernatural knowledge of God, we attempted to define it metaphysically by reference to the primary and secondary causality operative in man's existence. From one point of view, my active existence is exercised by me, its second cause: from another point of view by its first cause, God. My natural mind is identified with the operation of the second cause. In so far as I am made to see things in any degree as from within the operation of the first cause, my mind performs a supernatural act: and this cannot happen by my exertion, but by God's supernaturalizing action. Now the Person of Christ, in the belief of Catholic Christendom, is, as it were by definition, the height of supernaturality: for in it the first and second causes are personally united, the finite and infinite centres in some manner coincide; manhood is so taken into God, that the human life of Jesus is exercised from the centre of deity, so far as a human life on earth can be, without ceasing to be a human life on earth: for in him also the general maxim is verified—the supernatural enhances and intensifies, but does not remove nature.

Thus, as a matter of faith, we believe that the revelation of deity to manhood is absolutely fulfilled in Christ himself: in him, man exercises not a supernatural act only, but a supernatural existence, in perfection; he both knows and enacts deity in all his life and thought. To speak so of Christ is to give a deceptively precise description of an unfathomable mystery. We define him, as we define deity itself, by a coincidence of opposites. Deity, for example, is defined as Timeless Life, though with us all life is temporal process and cannot be imagined otherwise, and all that is timeless is lifeless abstraction and cannot be imagined otherwise. In much the

same manner we define Christ by the coincidence of supernaturalized manhood and self-bestowing deity, though with
us even supernaturalized manhood merely aspires after the
infinite transcendence of deity and cannot be imagined
otherwise, and even self-bestowing deity is the infinitely
distant goal of human aspiration and cannot be imagined
otherwise. Christ's Person defeats our intellect, as deity
defeats it, and for the same reason, for deity is in it. So the
sheer occurrence of Christ's existence is the perfection of
revelation to Man, but it is not yet the perfection, or
even the beginning of revelation to us, unless we are
enabled to apprehend the fathomless mystery which his
manhood is.

The first thing to be said of Christ's self-revelation to us is
that it is by word and deed, where 'doing' is taken to em-
brace the action of Christ's will in his *sufferings* also. If we are
allowed this gloss, we may be content with St. Luke's
formula: 'the things that Christ did and taught' are the
subject-matter of the gospel.

The actions of Christ's will, the expressions of his mind:
these, certainly, are the precious seeds of revelation, but they
are not the full-grown plant. Everything that grows must
grow from them: but the growth is as necessary as the seed, if
there is to be any fruit. It would be abstractly possible to conceive that Christ should have given in his teaching a sufficient
exposition of the saving mystery of his being and his act: but
even in a context of *a priori* argument we must deign to
acknowledge facts. The facts to be considered are two. First,
the New Testament itself tells us that the words of Christ in
the days of his flesh were not, without comment, sufficient to
reveal salvation. Second, our own historical study of the New
Testament leads to the conclusion that we cannot separate off
from apostolic comment a body of Christ's sayings which by
themselves surely and sufficiently determine saving truth. So
the apostolic church tells us that we cannot do without what
the Spirit revealed to the Apostles: and by study of the New

Testament we discover that we are lost, without what the Spirit revealed to the Apostles.

Such is the situation. It is often misleadingly expressed in a distinction between 'the fact of Christ' and 'the inspired apostolic comment', as though Christ has said nothing, and the apostles had done nothing. Christ both performed the primary action and gave the primary interpretation: the apostles, supernaturalized by the Spirit of Pentecost, worked out both the saving action and the revealing interpretation of Christ. As his action underlies theirs, so his interpretation underlies theirs. It is not my reading of the biblical evidence that the luxuriant growth of apostolic teaching is impenetrable—that it utterly hides Jesus, the root from which it springs. I will freely confess, for my own part, that unless I thought myself honestly led to recognize in Christ's historical teaching seeds of the doctrine of his divine person and work, then I should not believe. I cannot take these things simply from St. Peter and St. Paul, as their inspired reaction to 'the fact of Christ'. But I can accept St. Peter's and St. Paul's inspired comment as the absolutely necessary guide to what I may recover of the Lord's own oracles. Again, if I did not, in my own judgment, consider that the Lord's oracles bore out the apostolic comment, I should not believe. But that does not mean that apart from the apostolic record, I could from the bare oracles make out the apostolic doctrine for myself. I could not.

The work of revelation, like the whole work of Christ, is the work of the mystical Christ, who embraces both Head and members. But, as in other aspects of his work, the action of the Head must be central and primary, it must contain in epitome all that the members fulfil and spread abroad. The primacy of the Head in revelation is seen in two things. First, the self-giving of the divine mind to man is fully actualized in the personal existence of Jesus Christ. Secondly, the communication to mankind in general of the human-divine mind of Jesus Christ is begun by Jesus Christ, who by that beginning lays down the lines of all further development. Development is development, and neither addition nor alteration. The first and decisive development is the work of the Apostolic age.

The interpretative work of the Apostles must be understood as participation in the mind of Christ, through the Holy Ghost: they are the members, upon whom inflows the life of the Head. As the ministerial action of Christ is extended in the Apostolic Mission, so the expressed thought of Christ is extended in the Apostolic teaching. Now the thought of Christ Himself was expressed in certain dominant images. He spoke of the Kingdom of God, which is the image of God's enthroned majesty. In some sense, he said, the regal presence and power was planted on earth in his own presence and action: in some other sense its advent was still to be prayed for: in some sense men then alive should remain to witness its coming. Again, he spoke of the Son of Man, thereby proposing the image of the dominion of a true Adam, begotten in the similitude of God, and made God's regent over all the works of his hands. Such a dominion Christ claimed to exercise in some manner there and then: yet in another sense it was to be looked for thereafter, when the Son of Man should come with the clouds of heaven, seated at the right hand of Almightiness. He set forth the image of Israel, the human family of God, somehow mystically contained in the person of Jacob, its patriarch. He was himself Israel, and appointed twelve men to be his typical 'sons'. He applied to himself the prophecies of a redemptive suffering for mankind attributed to Israel by Isaiah and Jewish tradition. He displayed, in the action of the supper, the infinitely complex and fertile image of sacrifice and communion, of expiation and covenant.

These tremendous images, and others like them, are not the whole of Christ's teaching, but they set forth the supernatural mystery which is the heart of the teaching. Without them, the teaching would not be supernatural revelation, but instruction in piety and morals. It is because the spiritual instruction is related to the great images, that it becomes revealed truth. That God's mind towards his creatures is one of paternal love, is a truth almost of natural religion and was already a commonplace of Judaism. That God's paternal love takes action in the gift of the Kingdom through the death of the Son of Man, this is supernatural revelation.

The great images interpreted the events of Christ's ministry, death and resurrection, and the events interpreted the images; the interplay of the two is revelation. Certainly the events without the images would be no revelation at all, and the images without the events would remain shadows on the clouds. The events by themselves are not revelation, for they do not by themselves reveal the divine work which is accomplished in them: the martyrdom of a virtuous Rabbi and his miraculous return are not of themselves the redemption of the world.

The interplay of image and event continues in the existence of the apostles. As the divine action continues to unfold its character in the descent of the Spirit, in the apostolic mission, and in the mystical fellowship, so the images given by Christ continue to unfold within the apostolic mind, in such fashion as to reveal the nature of the supernatural existence of the apostolic church. In revealing the Church, they of necessity reveal Christ also, and the saving work he once for all performed. For the supernatural life of the Church can be no more than the exposition in the members of the being of their Head. If they understand their life-in-grace, they understand the grace by which they live, and that grace is Christ's saving work. St. Paul, for example, sees that his own life in Christ is a continual death and resurrection: and in understanding so his own living exposition of Christ's redemption, he of necessity understands the redemption of which it is the exposition.

In the apostolic mind, we have said, the God-given images lived, not statically, but with an inexpressible creative force. The several distinct images grew together into fresh unities, opened out in new detail, attracted to themselves and assimilated further image-material: all this within the life of a generation. This is the way inspiration worked. The stuff of inspiration is living images.

It is surely of high importance to know what is to be looked for in Scripture. The Mediaeval Scholastic mind, it would seem, was (in theory, at any rate) on the hunt for theological propositions, out of which a correct system of doctrine could be deduced by logical method. If we set about the quest in that way, we close our ears to the voice of Scripture. The modern tendency is to seek after historical record, whether it be the record of events, or of spiritual states in apostolic minds: it is not surprising if it fails to find either the voice of God, or the substance of supernatural mystery. We have to listen to the Spirit speaking divine things: and the way to appreciate his speech is to quicken our own minds with the life of the inspired images.

I have heard it wisely said that in Scripture there is not a line of theology, and of philosophy not so much as an echo. Theology is the analysis and criticism of the revealed images: but before you can turn critic or analyst, you need a matter of images to practise upon. Theology tests and determines the sense of the images, it does not create it. The images, of themselves, signify and reveal.

Let us take an example of the way in which a matter of divine truth is contained in Scripture under the form of images. It is a famous question whether, and in what sense, the doctrine of the Trinity is in the New Testament. The answers which we get follow from our methods of putting the question. The old scholastic way was to hunt for propositions which declare or imply the doctrine in its philosophical form. It is possible to make out a case along these lines, but then along these lines it is possible to make out a case for most things. Then there is the new scholastic way, the method of the research-degree thesis. We painfully count and classify all the texts in St. Paul or St. John in which the Heavenly Father, the Divine Son and the Holy Ghost are mentioned, either severally or in connexion with one another. We inquire whether the texts about the Second and Third Persons talk of them as personally presenting deity, or not: and what is implied of their relation to the First Person and to one another.

This method, since it starts from statistics and lexicography, exercises the usual fascination of those techniques over our minds: but it is false in its assumptions and inconclusive in its results. It is false in its assumptions, because it supposes that St. Paul or St. John is, after all, a systematic theologian. A very unsystematic systematic theologian, no doubt, too impulsive and enthusiastic to put his material in proper order or to standardize his terminology. Still, what of that? Anyone who has a decent modern education can do it for him: we, for example, will be rewarded a research degree for doing it. We will draw into the light the system which was coming to birth in the Apostle's mind. But suppose there was no system coming to birth in the Apostle's mind at all—not, that is, on the conceptual level? Suppose that his thought centred round a number of vital images, which lived with the life of images, not of concepts. Then each image will have its own conceptual conventions, proper to the figure it embodies: and a single over-all conceptual analysis will be about as useful for the interpretation of the Apostle's writings as a bulldozer for the cultivation of a miniature landscape-garden. The various images are not, of course, unconnected in the Apostle's mind, they attract one another and tend to fuse, but they have their own way of doing this, according to their own imagery laws, and not according to the principles of conceptual system.

The method of the research-degree thesis is inconclusive in its results, because it attempts to find the Trinity as a single scheme behind the many images. But here we break down for lack of evidence. It is obvious, before we start, and without the statistics or the lexicography, that St. Paul's several imagery statements speak of personal divine action in the Father, the Son, and the Holy Ghost, and further, that St. Paul was not a polytheist. But whether he regards the Son and the Spirit as instrumental modes of the Father's action, or as divine Persons in their own right, can be determined only by a subtle and risky construction of inferences. Just because St. Paul writes in images, we fall into absurdity at the first inferential step. Have we not been taught that images can be trusted only to express what he who speaks them intends by them, and that if we syllogize from them in the direction of our own questions which are not his, our process is completely invalid: like that of the man who asks what is the meaning of details in a parable having no bearing on what the speaker has used the parable to say. 'Straightway he puts in the sickle, because the harvest is come.' The reaper is the Son of Man, the corn is the faithful: what does the sickle represent?

A third method of enquiry fastens on the subjective form of religious experience. St. Paul's images, after all, it is said, are but the expression in various figures of his existence in grace. Let us try to strip the images down and get to the experience of grace which underlies. Surely, then, we may say, St. Paul is aware of the grace of creation—he experiences God as the fount of his being: he therefore acknowledges the Father. He experiences also the grace of Christ—he knows the human-divine life, now ascended, with which he is bound up in one body of supernatural action, as the hand is related to the head. Here is quite a different way of experiencing God —the experience of the Son. But again, there is the experience of holy possession—of being directly seized and filled with the divine life, of being operated by God—and that is the experience of the Holy Ghost. Very well: but here, once more, we break down at the crucial point. Here we have a triform experience of God, not the experience of a triune deity. If human existence is a prism which breaks the single ray of divine grace into several colours, that is just what we might expect: for it is universally true that our experience of God and our thought of God resolve the unity of the great Cause in the plurality of his effects.

A fourth method seeks after formulae. St. Matthew's gospel

requires baptism in the name of Father, Son and Holy Ghost: St. Paul once prays that the grace of the Lord Jesus, the love of God, and the communion of the Holy Ghost may be with the Church at Corinth: and he has a tendency, though not a very strong tendency, to print the pattern of God, Lord and Spirit on his homiletical paragraphs. Now this method does at least arrive at apostolic consciousness of a triad: but it does not tell us of what the triad is a triad. Whether it is a triad of Divine Persons or a triad of saving mysteries, we still do not know. Undoubtedly Christians were baptized into the family of the divine Father, centred in the sonship of Jesus Christ, and cemented by the mystery of indwelling: we do not need the formula to tell us that. But do they tell us any more than that?

If we want to find the Divine Trinity in the New Testament, we must look for the image of the Divine Trinity. We must look for it as a particular image, here or there. Most of the time other images will be occupying the page: we must be content if we can find it anywhere. Our next endeavour, after we have found it, must be to isolate it and distinguish it from other images, not to show that other images are really expressed in terms of it, for they are not. The Trinity is one of the images that appear, it is not a category of general application. When we have isolated the image of the Trinity, and studied it in itself, we can then proceed to ask what place it occupies in the world of New Testament images—whether dominant or subordinate, vital or inessential: and how other images are affected by it. After that we can, if we like, go on to ask what metaphysical comment the New Testament image of the Trinity provokes, and which subsequent theological conceptualizations do least violence to it.

But is the image of the Trinity in the New Testament? The image we have to look for is that of a divine Son pre-existing in heaven and bound to his Heavenly Father by the Father's Spirit. Such an image can certainly be found. It is, indeed, a pre-Christian image, except that the Son is neither divine nor really pre-existent, in the pre-Christian form of it. We may start with the eleventh chapter of Isaiah, in which we read of an anointed king, whose anointing is not with oil, but with the Spirit of the Lord, resting sevenfold upon him. Here are the elements of the Trinitarian image. We may take as the next step forward a text which overlays the idea of spiritual anointing with the idea of divine sonship. A famous Jewish writing, known to the principal New Testament authors, is 'the Testaments of the XII Patriarchs'. This book looks forward to a supreme anointed head, of whom it writes: 'For him the heavens will be opened, and there will descend hallowing upon him, with the Father's voice as from Abraham to Isaac.' The author goes on to set forth the 'hallowing' as the Holy Spirit, in words which are a direct allusion to the eleventh chapter of Isaiah. 'The Father's voice as from Abraham to Isaac' is the voice of the Father upraised in blessing upon an only and beloved Son: 'only and beloved son' being the unforgettable and repeated designation of Isaac in the most memorable history about him. We may now advance into the New Testament itself, to see the whole image become fact in the baptism of Jesus Christ. The heavens are now opened indeed, the voice of the Father audibly designates a divine Isaac as his beloved Son, and the spirit of hallowing descends visibly as a dove.

This is what we read in St. Mark. The son is now divine, but is his association with the Father through the Father's Spirit yet seen as pre-existent and heavenly? What St. Mark describes takes place at the baptism of Christ: it is an earthly and historical event. Yes: though St. Mark, I do not doubt, saw the historical event as the temporal manifestation of a state of things older than the world. But this does not become explicit in his Trinitarian image. For explicit development we must look elsewhere.

There is no doubt, anyhow, that the Son of the Johannine writings was Son before the world began. St. John sees him in his Apocalypse like a Lamb standing as slaughtered, having seven horns and seven eyes, which are the seven spirits of God;

they are the Holy Ghost, manifested as sevenfold vision and sevenfold strength. There is once more a plain allusion in the wording of the vision to Isaiah's oracle on the prince endowed sevenfold with the Spirit of the Lord. But, what is more significant, St. John has himself a few lines before described to us the same sevenfold Spirit of God as a cluster of seven flames burning before the Father's throne. The sevenfold light of the Holy Ghost burns before the Father's majesty, it blazes also in the eyes of the mystical Lamb. The Father's sevenfold plenitude of Spirit is bestowed upon the Son: 'he giveth not him the Spirit by measure.' The Father, the sevenfold Spirit before his throne, the Son on whom the whole Spirit is bestowed—this is the divine Trinity of Names wherewith St. John blesses, when he blesses in the Name of God: 'Grace to you and peace from the IS, WAS, and COMETH, and from the Seven Spirits that are before his throne, and from Jesus Christ, the Faithful Witness. . . .'

St. John simply sets forth the image of the Trinity as representing the mystery of divine love into which we are taken up. It is there before we are taken up into it: it belongs, it would seem, to the nature of things. It is plain that the seer does not intend to talk about the form of his own religious experience, but about a transcendent mystery which is simply there. It is because it is simply there, that it gives form to his experience. St. John is content to set forth the image. He does not speculatively determine the relation of the Son to the Father. Later theology was to conclude that there is no real meaning in the absolute priority and essentiality of Christ's sonship, if he is himself a creature. He must be himself of the deity. It must be that by an unfathomable mystery, Godhead itself moves round to face in filial devotion the paternal throne of Godhead, and to receive the indwelling of the Father through his inbreathed Spirit.

But that is to go beyond St. John, and beyond any New Testament text. We have in St. John simply the *image* of the Father, Son and Spirit, placed by relation to us and our salvation in the transcendent place he assigns it. We can argue if we like that it is no more than an hyperbole for the unique spiritual eminence of the man Jesus Christ: we can argue as we will: in any case the image is there, and it is the image out of which the dogma of the Trinity historically grew.

If we wish to determine the sense of the image beyond what it bears on its face, we must no doubt consider its relation to other Johannine images, not of themselves Trinitarian at all. For example, the image of Christ as the Word through whom God made the worlds. We shall have to consider the light thrown by the Word-image on the Trinitarian image, for both belong to the same apostolic mind. But we must, in comparing them, remember that they are distinct images: we must not force them to the pattern of one another. Such forcing was done by the Fathers of the Church, with tragic and confusing effects on Trinitarian speculation. The text about the Word occupies a position of special prominence at the beginning of St. John's Gospel. Here, if anywhere, thought the Fathers, Scripture offers us a summary of Christian metaphysics. The Trinity, they argued, is the chief article of Christian metaphysical belief, so the Trinity must be here. What, then, does the text say?

'In the beginning was the Word, and the Word was with God, and the Word was God.

'He was in the beginning with God; through him all things arose, and without him arose nothing.

'What arose through him was life, and the life was the light of men.'

This life, which arose through the Word, must clearly be the Holy Ghost, the Fathers thought: and so we have the doctrine that the Holy Ghost proceeds from the Father through the Son. But this doctrine not only falsifies the scriptural image of the Trinity, it also makes any doctrine of an eternal Trinity unintelligible. For by the Spirit Scripture understands only one thing, the life of the Godhead as bestowed. Bestowed, then, on whom? Bestowed *now* on redeemed mankind—'the life was the light of men'. But that will not give us an eternal Trinity above all worlds, but only a Trinitarian disposition of the Godhead for the salvation of the world. A Spirit eternally bestowed requires an eternal and adequate recipient. According to the Trinitarian images of St. Mark and St. John, this recipient is the divine Son. The Son is eternally begotten, and the Spirit is eternally inbreathed into him by the lips of his begetter. The act of paternal love is two-fold—to beget and to bestow. Such is the divine life above all worlds: when we, by unspeakable mercy, are taken up to partake in it, we partake in both the begetting and the gift. Christ's sonship is extended to us, his spiritual anointing over-flows upon us. All this we see in the clarity of the image. But the Fathers, who did not consistently respect the method of images, were bound to force and confuse the sense of scripture. One could not easily find a more telling example of the vital importance of the principle, that images are the stuff of revelation, and that they must be interpreted according to their own laws.

The theologian may confuse the images, and the meta-physician may speculate about them; but the Bible-reader will immerse himself in the single image on the page before him, and find life-giving power in it, taken as it stands. He reads how we were bondmen until God 'sent forth his Son, born of a woman . . . that we might receive the adoption of sons': and how, to confirm our sonship, there was a second mission: 'God sent forth the Spirit of his Son into our hearts, crying Abba, Father.' The Christian who reads this con-siders the perfection of unique divine sonship, and stirs his heart to gratitude for the amazing gift of a share in it: he awes his mind with the thought that he is possessed by the Spirit of God, and is, in reality and in God's eyes, Christ towards his God and towards his neighbour: he deplores the darkness which commonly veils what now he sees in the clarity of faith, and the sin which falsifies it in act. He throws himself on the love of the Trinity, more patient with him than he is with himself, and silently operative to produce in him even such penitence and vision as now he has. All these motions of the soul take place within the field of the image: they do not pass out of it into the thin upper air of definition and speculation, nor down onto the flat ground of mere penitence and self-management.

Now it will be said, and rightly said, that however vital a place great images hold in the text of the New Testament, they by no means fill it all. Thus, to say that the apostolic mind was divinely inspired by the germination there of the image-seeds which Christ had sown, is not to give a plain and uniform account of the inspiration of the text of Scripture, comparable with the old doctrine of inerrant supernatural dictation. But this, surely, is no blemish. For a doctrine of the unchallengeable inspiration of the whole text is a burden which our backs will no longer bear. What is vital is that we should have such a doctrine of Scripture as causes us to look for the right things in reading Scripture: above all, that we should look for the life-giving inspired word, and make the proper use of it when we have found it. There is a great deal else in Scripture. If we want a single formula to cover the unique value of it all, then it seems we must call it not 'inspired' but 'revealing', in the sense of 'informative about saving facts': for it contains historical matter, and matter which, not itself historical, is of predominantly historical interest to us: for example, St. Paul's direct discussion of certain practical problems which have no close analogy in our own world, but cast a vivid light on the primitive community.

Yet, as soon as we have made the distinction between the 'informative' and the 'inspired', we feel inclined to retract it. For the effects of inspiration are widely seen over the historical paragraphs, and anything which suggests the fencing-off of non-inspired areas is to be abhorred. For example, it used to be thought, some twenty years ago, by people who ought to have known better, that St. Mark's gospel is informative rather than inspired, that it is a patient and somewhat unhandy compilation of traditions, rather than an inspired interpretation. We know better now. Inspired image and historical memory are so fused in this oldest of our gospels, that it is virtually impossible any more to pull them apart. Or to take St. Paul's discussions of practical problems, now obsolete. How long does he ever remain on the simply practical plane? Do not we, as we read, suddenly perceive that the apostle's feet have gone through the floor and his head through the roof, and that he is speaking in the large dimension of inspired vision? Presently, in the authority and the spirit of a great image, he returns to settle the matter in hand.

It might do justice to the facts as we see them, if we described Scripture as 'a body of writings uniquely informative, and a field in which inspiration works'. And that description may stand, even though we must proceed to take a further distinction within the work of inspiration. Where, we may ask, does the act of inspiration take place? Does it take place in the mind of the biblical writer as he composes, or rather at other times, say in prayer and worship, or even in other men, for example, in prophets and possessors of various 'spiritual gifts?' And if so, is the biblical writer to be regarded as retailing inspiration in the images he employs, rather than undergoing it there and then?

We cannot return a simple answer to this question. On the one hand, we cannot think of reviving the old biblicist error, always, perhaps, more common as an unexamined assumption than as a consciously held belief. We cannot say that the primary instrument of the Pentecostal Spirit was the Bible. No, it was the apostolic Church, of which the apostles and prophets were the sensitive organs. If the biblical books had not been taken to express the apostolic mind, they would not have been canonized: and we shall rightly suppose that the dominant images of the New Testament were the common property of the teaching Church. But it would be mistaken to infer that direct and immediate inspiration played a small part in the composition of the books. It may be that the decisive shaping of the images took place elsewhere. But the images are still alive and moving in the writers' minds, not fixed or diagrammatic. They continue to enter into fresh combinations, to elaborate themselves, to beget new applications. The composition of the books may be on the fringe of the great process of inspired thinking, but it is still inspired thinking, much of it as vivid and forcible as anything one could well conceive.

We have to remember that the business of writing about sacred matters was viewed by the Jew with a solemnity which we cannot easily recover. There was for him only one primary body of writings, the sacred scriptures of the Old Testament: any other writing must be regarded as a sort of extension of Scripture, and he who composed it must attempt to draw out the substance of scripture by spiritual aid. The New Testament writers are given a position of greater independence through the new revealing acts of God, but that will not alter at once the spirit in which they approach their task. St. Mark's and St. John's Gospels, and St. John's Apocalypse, are, by their very *genre*, sacred writings, mysteries. It is often said that it would have amazed these writers to learn that their books would be viewed as 'Scripture'. I believe this to be true only in so restricted a sense, that it is, if taken without qualification, a pernicious error. They would have been surprised to see their books treated as *primary* scripture, and placed on a level with the Old Testament. But that they were writing books of the *nature* of sacred scripture, they did not doubt: they had no idea of doing anything else. And so it is virtually certain that, if they were men capable of inspired thinking, they did it then, with their pens in their hands.

The case of the Epistles, or anyhow of those Epistles which really were letters written upon particular occasion to a particular address, is not quite the same: but to suggest that they were simply letters of the sort one writes every day, is grossly absurd. They are at the very least instruments of sacred teaching and authoritative apostolic direction. If St. Paul invoked

the spirit of prophecy when he spoke mighty and burning
words in the congregation, so he might when he composed
the letter which was to be read out as his voice's substitute. In
fact he records the opinion of some, that he was weightier
with his pen than with his lips. Nor would he suppose for a
moment that the Corinthian or Philippian Church, after
reading his inspired admonition, would toss it into the fire.
They would keep it by them (as they did) to be an enduring
guide. Many students of scripture might incline to judge that
the breath of high inspiration blows more unevenly in St.
Paul's true Epistles than anywhere else in the New Testament.
When it comes upon him, he achieves sublimities nowhere
else found: when the mood or the subject is more pedestrian,
so is the level of his writing.

The New Testament books may not be at the centre of the
process of Pentecostal inspiration, but they are our only direct
clue to its nature, and if we neglect the evidence they supply,
we shall know nothing about it. It is the constant experience
of him who studies the records of the past, that he begins by
reading ancient books for the light they cast on the minds of
those about whom they write, and then comes to realize that
the only mind with which they bring him into immediate
and satisfying contact is the mind of their author. We may
read the New Testament for what it tells us about prophetic
inspiration through the Spirit of Pentecost, in the hope of
constructing some account of the phenomenon. But what we
learn is little but externals: that the Spirit appeared to act
compulsively, that prophets had difficulty in withholding
their utterance until suitable occasion, that they supposed
themselves to be the heirs of the Israelite prophets and imi-
tated their behaviour, that it was taken for granted by all that
they were really possessed, that tests were applied to prove
whether their possession was of God or Beelzebub, that some
of their utterances were particular predictions, and others of
them rebukes which laid bare the innermost thoughts of their
hearers. All this is of interest so far as it goes, but it does not

tell us what sort of yeast it was that worked in those exalted minds: indeed, we are tempted to complain that the primitive Christians were too much impressed by the froth. No doubt what they called prophecy was often frothy enough. But the true substance of inspiration was surely everywhere one: the most histrionic of the prophets, if they had any breath of real inspiration in them, were under the pressure of supernatural mysteries speaking through living images. If we want to know anything of the nature of the process, we must see how the minds of the sacred writers are moved as they write, in their passages of high inspiration.

Through the secret act of God by which the Apostles were inspired there came upon us in imaged presentation the shape of the mystery of our redemption. It possessed and moulded their minds, it possesses and moulds ours: we are taken up into the movement of the life above all creatures, of the Son towards the Father in the Holy Ghost. *Now therefore and always be ascribed as is most justly due all might, dominion, majesty and power to the Unity indivisible, the Trinity of sovereign love.*

IV

And God said unto Moses: I am that I am.

EXODUS, III. 14

We have concluded that divine truth is supernaturally communicated to men in an act of inspired thinking which falls into the shape of certain images. We have now to consider a further point: how it is that the images are able to signify divine realities. The images themselves are not what is principally revealed: they are no more than instruments by which realities are to be known. The inspired man may not reflect on the instrumental function of the images, but whether he reflects on it or not, he makes an instrumental use of them. He does not think *about* the images, but about what he takes them to signify. When a man speaks metaphorically without being aware of it, he is always attending to what the metaphor means, never to the metaphor. Conscious attention jumps the metaphor, but that does not make the role of the metaphor any less vital. Metaphors may mislead us or send us right, without our observing it. It is therefore always a question for a philosopher, whether a man using a given metaphor can be thinking to any purpose with such a metaphor about such a subject.

Suppose, for example, I were to say to you: 'It stands to reason that the stronger of two desires must prevail with me, unless a third force of some kind intervenes.' Would you not retort with one voice that I am abusing a metaphor? That I am symbolizing the will as a physical field in which commensurable forces of ascertainable strengths collide: that the metaphor has its uses, but is childishly inadequate, and that the inward experience of ourselves nowhere shows us such commensurable and determinate forces of desire: that the conclusion I draw follows from the structure of the symbol I use, not from the structure of the reality it symbolizes. And if I cry out for mercy, and say I was not even aware of using any metaphorical symbol at all, you will pitilessly insist 'So much the worse: if you had criticized your images, you would not have talked such nonsense'.

Thus the fact that St. Paul or St. John is inspired through the working of images to think divine mysteries under the images, does not foreclose the question, how thinking of such a type can express truth, or why we should accept it as true. We have not here merely the common risks of metaphorical discourse to reckon with: we have a special difficulty which is far worse, and of which the nature is fairly obvious. For we suppose in general that the applicability of images is to be tested by looking away from the images to the things they symbolize, as in the difficult example we were considering just now. It might be hard, by self-analysis, to see how the lure of any desire operated, but anyhow there was hope of our being able to make out enough of even so baffling an object, to decide whether the gross physical analogy of measurable impelling force applied or no. So far so good. But in the case of supernatural divine revelation, nothing but the image is given us to act as an indication of the reality. We cannot appeal from the images to the reality, for by hypothesis we have not got the reality, except in the form of that which the images signify.

But have not we got the reality? Does God feed his saints with nothing but figures of speech? Does he not also operate in their souls the supernatural action to which the figures refer? St. John is inspired to think of the incarnation under the figure of a word of power clothing itself in flesh and blood. But along with the figurative declaration of the incarnation, does not God breathe into him the substance and act of the incarnation? Is not God's incarnation operative in the members as well as the head, in John as well as in the manhood of Jesus Christ? Does not John exercise supernatural virtue, does not he pray in the heart of Jesus Christ, is not his charity carried and moved by Christ? And if so, can he not refer the figurative description of the incarnation to the experienced act of the incarnation, and judge the adequacy of the expression by awareness of the thing expressed?

The question we have asked does not admit of a yes-or-no answer. On the one hand it must be admitted that apart from the presence in the soul of a foretaste or earnest of supernatural life, revealed truth is dumb to us. We may hear and read the verbal declaration of divine truth for years, and not apprehend the thing signified; when a motion of supernatural life stirs within us, then we have thing as well as word, and begin to apprehend. But on the other hand it is an absurdity to suggest that the supernatural action we exercise is the adequate real counterpart of the divine truth we believe. There is no sort of proportion between the two. What is, as an exercised act, the least kindling of supernatural charity, the slightest uplifting of the heart towards God, is interpreted by faith as the extension of God's Incarnation, the indwelling of the Godhead in the Person of the Holy Ghost, the effect of an eternal predestination, and the beginning of our everlasting divinization. Are all these mighty mysteries adequately expressed in our supernatural act? Are they expressed there at all?

We are faced here with as delicate an issue of definition as any that is ever likely to meet us. In trying to deal with it, we shall probably find ourselves beginning from spatial metaphor, as we commonly do. We shall say something like this: 'The total object in which we believe is a vast divine process, in the Godhead, in the manhood of Christ, in the whole mystical body of Christ. A part of this process takes place within any one believer at any given time: but how infinitesimal a part! It bears no proportion at all to what takes place outside him. To suppose that we can judge of the whole by the infinitesimal part is absurd: our picture of the whole must be supernaturally imprinted on us, and supernaturally interpreted to us: we cannot interpret so much from so little, the whole blaze of divine action from the faint spark it kindles in ourselves.'

Such a line of reflection may carry conviction while we entertain it: but presently it will provoke a reaction. What is this ungodly nonsense, we exclaim, about areas of divine process outside us and within us, as though the proportion between them were to be taken in square yards? Is not our faith precisely this, that the *whole* Christ is active in associating our life with his, and that the Holy Ghost personally indwells us? Is Christ divided? Can the Person of the Spirit be parcelled out? The whole mystery, not a part of it, is active at each point. To apprehend that single point, then, is to apprehend the substance of the whole mystery. And so there is no reason why the supernatural act wrought in us should not suffice as the real and directly known object, to which the revealed figurative description may be referred.

Very well, and the conclusion is proper enough so far as a complete view of the facts is concerned. The divine mind could construe the whole saving mystery from the single supernatural act in any soul: but then the divine mind does not need to, for it also sees the whole operation of the mystery direct, for it sees all things. But, for our minds, a curtain hangs between the divine agency and its effect in us. We may be directly aware of the supernatural in the form of our own supernatural act: but we are not in the same way aware of the divine agency effecting it in us. Though the divine agent be nearer to our act than the fleshly body our act indwells, a subtle veil secludes him, of no thickness, yet impenetrably dark. Were it to rend, that would be the Day of Judgment, for we should see our Creator.

Yet on further reflection we shall rebel against the veil-image too: it is as misleading as any other. How, we shall ask, can our supernatural act be so utterly secluded from the knowledge of its divine context? For if it were, it would not have the subjective form of a supernatural act. The act by which we love God is an intentional act, and intentional acts take their natures from the objects upon which their intentions are directed: and the intention cannot be directed unless the object is known. The supernatural act of love is not merely directed upon God, for in that case a natural apprehension of God might suffice, without revelation. It is directed upon God revealed in the act of his incarnation. Our supernatural act is precisely the love of a God revealed: and so the veil is done away, for we cannot love him unless we know him.

Yes, but we can love a God whom we know by faith alone; and therefore the veil remains. All we have to say is that the veil, however impenetrable, is not blank. It is painted with the image of God, and God himself painted it, and made it indelible with his blood, when he was nailed to it for us men and for our salvation. We know him through the image, and by faith: our supernatural acts take their intention and form from a revealed description of the saving mysteries. Thus, to say that we perceive in our own supernatural act the reality to which the revealed figures refer, is an absurdity: our act embodies in itself the form of the mysteries, but only by believing in them through the revealed figures. Faith must recognize in the supernatural human act not the reality of which she apprehends the image, but a fresh reflection of the image of herself: charity is faith reflected into action. Yet again the figure misleads us; for as compared with the images faith perceives, our supernatural act of charity is not more shadowy, the shadow of a shadow: it is more substantial, the process of the retranslation from shadow into substance has begun. The act of believing charity is a real supernatural effect, a part of the great mystical action, and a foretaste of the beatific vision.

It is unnecessary for us to carry the dialectics of faith and knowledge any further. What we have said is sufficient to establish what we have to shew. The supernatural act in man is a foretaste of the whole substance of the saving mystery, as he will behold it in the beatific vision, but it is no more than a foretaste: and if we set it alongside the figures of revelation, we must say that there is a huge overplus of sheer promise in what the figures express. The paradox remains. How can we receive and understand a promise, unless we know by experience the things promised? We need not, of course, know just those things, but things of the same sort, we surely must know. The child has never been to the party where you promise to take him: but to parties he has been. We have not 'seen' God at any time. How, then, can we understand the figures that speak of him?

The question which the paradox drives us to ask, is this: Can metaphorical images be understood in no way but by getting behind them to a non-metaphorical understanding of fact? Can it be that images themselves and by themselves are able to illuminate us? The suggestion appears at first sight logically scandalous, but we are reduced to such straits that we must examine it, however unpromising it may appear. After all, we may fairly doubt whether our commonsense logical assumptions really do justice to the part played by images in our thinking.

If we are to consider this question, we shall not be wise to take it up at the level where we are now standing, that is, the level of revelation and faith. Revelation may present the extreme example of irreducible imagery, but it will scarcely present the most manageable example. Rational Theology will be a more hopeful starting-point: and we seem to remember having heard that the rational knowledge of God comes to us wholly by way of analogies: and what are analogies but sober and criticized images?

Shall we start our enquiry, then, from Rational Theology? That may be an awkward thing to do, for '(Rational) Theology is accounted a part of (metaphysical) philosophy', and its method will presumably be no more than a special case of metaphysical method. We had better examine first the role of images in metaphysics. Even this will be no comfortable starting-point, for anyone who knows how the name of metaphysics sounds now in philosophical ears will realize into what a thicket of thorns we have run.

When a subject has become extremely perplexed, it is sometimes useful to draw back out of it, to view it as from a distance, and to speak of it with the greatest possible simplicity. And this is what I shall try to do about the matter of metaphysical philosophy. I listen to the debate which the philosophers sustain about the very possibility of metaphysics, and I try to strike a balance. The extreme enemies of metaphysics deny that any metaphysical proposition has any factual significance: the friends of metaphysics defend it as a meaningful way of thinking, but for the most part abandon the old account of it as a science in which exact problems about the real world arise, and obtain exact solutions. After listening to the debate, I feel that the ground of metaphysical thinking really is shifting. The world is not going to be persuaded that the whole business of metaphysics is without factual significance: but neither is the old 'science' of metaphysics going to be reinstated. What I shall advance in the following pages is little better than a parable. In such a matter as this, can a parable cast more light than it causes misunderstanding? Anyhow, let us take up our parable and speak.

There are, properly speaking, no metaphysical problems and no metaphysical solutions. There is, for example, no problem in finite causality to which the postulation of a divine First Cause is the solution. The business of metaphysics is not with problems but with mysteries, and mysteries are not to be solved, but (always inadequately) to be described. The so-called problems of metaphysics are difficulties of description: that does not make them either unimportant, or easy to manage. On the contrary, they may be quite agonizing; nor are any questions of greater importance to a mind which desires to understand the nature of its real world. There is no finality about the descriptions offered by metaphysics for the mysteries of existence, but there is advance in apprehension of the mysteries by the refining of the descriptions.

I shall now explain the difference between problems and mysteries, for the purposes of the present argument. The mysteries I shall speak of will not include all mysteries—not, for example, supernatural mysteries; but only the mysteries of our natural existence. And the problems I shall speak of will not include all problems, not for example, practical problems; but only the sort of problems most likely to get confused with natural mysteries. I will take problems first.

A problem arises in so far as we approach the world with a fixed measuring instrument, whether of the literal and physical, or of the conceptual sort. Let us begin with the physical instrument. If I approach my physical environment with an actual yardstick, problems arise about what the measure in yards of each thing is, and how the yard-measurement of one thing stands mathematically related to that of another. I know exactly what the problems are, and how they are in principle to be solved, even though I cannot solve some of them here and now; for example, I cannot measure a given line because it is an irregular curve, and my yardstick is fixed and straight, or I cannot measure the height of a tree, because I cannot climb to the top of it. Such difficulties as these give rise to a new sort of problem—the problem of perfecting the instrument of measurement. The problem of measuring the irregular curve may be solved by the brilliant invention of a tape-measure, and the problem of measuring the tree by an instrument recording an angle, taken from the ground by eye at a given distance from the tree. Here, then, are two sorts of problems: problems about elements in environment arising from, and solved by, the use of the instrument; and problems about the instrument, which arise from its inadequacy to an observed need, and are solved by its development or variation. To the first sort of problem there is always *the right answer*: the measurement of a given plank in yards is just what it is. To the second sort of problem there is *a* right answer—several different instruments might do the job, but anyhow, here is one which will do it.

The same two sorts of problems arise if I approach the world not with a tangible, but with a conceptual instrument, for example, a determinate idea of physical cause. This gives rise to any number of problems in environment, for it leads one to ask, what is the cause of each particular physical event. Again, it leads to problems about the instrument: in the attempt to fix particular causes we are driven to formulate general causal rules, and so the instrument is elaborated. Not only may it be elaborated, it may be revolutionized: in using her causal concept, science comes to see that a fundamentally different concept will be more fertile in its application: and so cause itself comes to mean something different from what it did.

The field of the problematic is the field in which there are right answers: and it is the field of what is commonly called 'science'. The sciences are distinguished from one another by the different conceptual instruments they severally employ: and the real subject-matter of any science is whatever in our environment is amenable to measurement by the conceptual instrument of that science. The sciences yield real information about the world, but only in terms of their conceptual instruments. It is only the relation of real things or events to the instruments that is disclosed: it is only the relation of the size of things to a yard-measure which is discovered by the use of a yard-measure, and only the relation of the structure of real processes to the formulated pattern of causal uniformity, which is discovered by the use of the formula of causal uniformity. The information which we get is real, for all magnitudes bear a real relation to a yardstick, or we could not measure them by it: and physical processes have an aspect which genuinely corresponds to our concept of causal uniformity, or we could not interpret them by it. The information which we gain is real, but it is highly abstract or selective. When I approach my environment, yardstick in hand, I do not ask the general question 'What have we here?' or even 'What here is most important?' but always the narrow question 'What will my yardstick tell me about the things that are here?'

The true scientist is justly credited with a supreme respect for fact, that is to say for the real world upon which he makes his experiments. He will stubbornly refuse to record what his yardstick does not bring to light, or to construct in defiance of any least thing that it does. This is rightly called respect for fact: but it can scarcely be called respect for being. The scientist may feel the deepest respect for being also; he may go in constant amazement at the mysterious nature which the world must be supposed to have in itself, so as to be the sort of world which yields such complex and orderly responses to his yardstick method. But this amazement, this almost religious awe, does not find direct expression in his scientific activity; in so far as he entertains such feelings, he is more of a metaphysician than a pure scientist. That is only another way of saying, that as well as being a scientist, he is a man: and indeed, most scientists are human.

If we have to suppose a state of exclusive preoccupation with the yardstick business itself, to the exclusion of all sense for real being, we must view such a state with the gravest disquiet; it portends the death of the soul. For religion is based on respect for being—for God, yes, but only because God is seen to be uniquely worthy of it by a mind open to respect for being in general. Now if our experiencing of things and persons is limited to the trying on them of pre-arranged tests devised by ourselves, full respect for their being is excluded from the first. If we respect any being, we allow it to make its own impression, and, as it were, to formulate its own claims upon us. Just as a man confessing his sins cannot choose what he will confess, and what he will hide, but must confess all, because he is not making a judgment, but submitting to judgment: so a man who feels respect for any being cannot choose what he will explore and what ignore in the object of respect, but must give to his thoughts the most self-denying adaptability, ready to apply or improvise whatever thought-forms the nature of the object may require, if the aspects it insists on presenting are to be appreciated. He cannot even be content to appreciate every given aspect; he will endeavour to integrate the aspects in the unity of their being, for it is being, not the abstracted aspects of being, which is properly to be revered.

Where the attitude of almost passive respect combines with a rigorous demand for understanding, metaphysical activity will appear. Since no ready-formulated tests are to be applied, and no yardstick is presupposed, no determinate and soluble problems arise for the metaphysician: to his enquiries there are no 'right answers'. He is not faced with the limited and manageable relation which arises between a conceptual instrument and the object it is applied to: he is faced with the object itself, in its fullness: and the object meets him not as a cluster of problems but as a single though manifold mystery. His purpose is to understand it as well as he may. Since the human mind understands in the act of discourse, and not by simple intuition, to understand will be to describe. The metaphysician seeks to understand his mysteries in seeking to describe them.

But, you may object, here the preconceived verbal yardstick immediately returns after all. For nobody, attempting to *describe* an object, makes up a new vocabulary for the purpose there and then. I may invent a new term to *designate* an object of which I am already sufficiently aware, but by assigning it this new-fangled name I do not either *describe* it to myself, or help myself to get hold of its nature. So it is only by means of preconceived terms that the metaphysician will be able to describe: he must approach his object with a whole cupboardful of yardsticks.

Yes, certainly: but the way in which he differs from the scientist is in the way he uses them. The scientist insists on his chosen yardstick, the domain of his science is just whatever that stick can be used to measure. It is true that, as we saw, the scientist does modify his instrument to make it more serviceable, but always so as to extend or refine its actual use. He will go forward with his method: that is what makes him a scientist in any one science. But the metaphysician must not predetermine his choice of conceptual instrument: he must be willing to use such terms as his object appears to demand. He cannot, of course, approach the object and hold out to it a tray of words and ask it kindly to pick out its own description. His approach to the object means his being already talking about the object in whatever terms he has chanced to begin. But his endeavour to comprehend the object means an endeavour to improve on his description, to find better terms. In fact, the metaphysician's method is to keep breaking his yardsticks against the requirements of real truth. The method which thus aims at the comprehension of the reality of things is that method of which Plato said that it and it alone proceeded by smashing the suggestions it put forward. By continually breaking and bettering and breaking his descriptions the metaphysician refines his understanding of that which he tries to describe.

The mysteries of which the metaphysician discourses are all of a high generality, but each is unique. An example of such a mystery is the relation of a knowing act to the thing it knows, or the relation of the mind to the body. Each of these relations is of the highest generality—every cognitive act provides an instance of the relation of knowledge to its object, and every human act or state whatsoever provides an instance of the relation of mind to body. But each of these relations is unique —it is fairly obvious that the relation of a knowing act to a thing known is not an instance of any other sort of relation: it is its own sort. So also with the relation of the mind to the body. What can be said, then, about the unique? Can the unique be described? We do not have to sit idly asking whether it can be described, for we are describing it instinctively, before we begin to reflect. I do not need to read philosophers, or to philosophize myself, before I begin thinking of the knowing act as a sort of intellectual sight. That is to say, I describe the knowing intellect by the analogy of the seeing eye. Or to take the other example—I think of my mental self as the inhabitant of my body, as the possessor and manipulator of my body, as a specialized activity of my body's, as simply identical with my body. All these conflicting descriptions occur to me at different times, and all are analogies. The man's mind is to the man's body as the whole man is to his house—but it cannot be, for the relation of man to house is a relation of body to body, and how can the mind-body relation be like that? And so on with the rest.

What, then, does the metaphysician do? He does not simply reject all the analogies equally. He rejects the casual and fantastic, and holds fast those which seem most illuminating and natural. Into any analogy that he retains, he will gradually introduce more and more artificial modifications, for the purpose of suiting the analogy to the mysterious reality it is being used to describe. For example, the Aristotelian philosophy plainly describes the relation of the knowing act to the object known, by analogy with the relation of the exact replica of a thing to the thing of which it is the replica. We really begin with the formula, that for our act of intellect to know a mountain, is for it to *be* the mountain it knows, so that there is perfect correspondence between the known and the knowing of it. But so gross and violent an analogy would scarcely pass as a masterpiece of metaphysical description. The philosophers of the Aristotelian school show their wit in breaking down the analogy by a series of modifications. The knowing mind is the mountain—but not all of the mountain. It is the form of the mountain without the matter. For there are general aspects of the rocky mass in virtue of which we call it a mountain, and it is these aspects alone that the mind understands when it understands 'mountain'. So we have no need to import all those tons of variously-veined actual granite into the mind.

After all, the eye, from a distance, may be said to take the form of the mountain: and what the eye takes seems a highly etherialized and insubstantial sort of thing: so let us say that the form of the mountain, which the knowing mind 'becomes', is something like that. It still corresponds to something in the mountain, for the mountain really has the form. Yes, but it will never do, either, to say that the mind 'becomes' the *visible* form of the mountain, for then the mind would be the sense of sight, which it is not. It must become the *intelligible* form of the mountain, and that will be something still more subtle and immaterial. The visible form of mountain is always the form of one particular mountain: but the intelligible form is common to all mountains worthy of the name. When we have reached this point we have reached the point of metaphysical crisis. We have so whittled away and subtilized our original analogy, that it seems if we could subtilize a little further we should express the very mentality of mind: but on the other hand, if we did subtilize any further, we should run the risk of getting completely out of touch with the analogy from which we started: our pipe-line of analogical fuel would be drawn so fine that no substance of analogy would pass down it; in further refining the analogy we should be refining nothing, our refinement would mean nothing and would describe nothing. Thus, if we want to proceed further than the last stage of refinement our analogy will bear, we can only do it by standing on the extreme tip of our tapering spit of analogical description, and pointing out to sea. We say 'We are getting towards the nature of the knowing act, but still this isn't it: it is just itself, and lies beyond'.

Such dumb pointing is not, of course, the only resource of the metaphysician who has stretched his analogical tether to the limit. He may take up an alternative analogy for the same mystery, and work that out in a similar way; he may attempt a composite picture out of several analogies: there is no end to the things he may do. Nevertheless, in principle, the method remains what our sketch indicates: the description of natural mysteries by the criticism of analogies. And 'analogies' is only another name for sober and appropriate images.

When I talk thus about the business of metaphysics, I have my eyes fixed on the great metaphysicians of the past and consider what they have in fact been at: not what they say they have been at, but what I see them to have been at. If someone now wishes to give the name of metaphysics a new sense, he is no doubt free to do so: let him confine metaphysics to the criticism of our own intellectual presuppositions, and exclude it from pronouncing on the truth of things. It will remain that the great metaphysicians of the past wrestled to describe the real; he who admitted himself to have nothing to say about reality acknowledged himself to be no metaphysician.

But, by this very test, that is, by the practice of the great metaphysicians, is not our own account of metaphysics refuted? It might fairly be objected that what we have hitherto discussed under the name is not metaphysics at all, but something else—let us call it desultory dialectic, or free existential description. For, so far as our account has gone, metaphysics might be a gallery of miscellaneous analogical pictures representing each a separate 'mystery', and each worked out in a distinct technique, according to the requirements of its subject. Is this metaphysics? Surely metaphysics begins with the endeavour to unite the several pictures into one panorama, one interlocking system of all the mysteries.

If he is to achieve the unity of system, the metaphysician must select certain analogies of supreme common usefulness and apply them everywhere, not, of course, with the yardstick uniformity of scientific concepts, but variously broken down and qualified to suit the several spheres of their application. It was this that Aristotle was in fact doing when he interpreted the knowing act as an event in which the mind becomes the form of the object known. When we discussed this example just now, we talked as though Aristotle had adopted his terms of description in an unprejudiced attempt to appreciate the knowing act on its own merits: that is to say, we talked as though Aristotle were engaged in free existential description. But he was not: he was working within a system of which the analogical conventions were already fixed before he approached the mystery of the knowing act: they had been already fixed by his analysis of physical being and physical change. There was no question of his abandoning these basic conventions: the only question was, how they must be broken down and manipulated to express the special character of the knowing act.

At the first glance, it may seem folly for the metaphysician thus to tie his hands. If his business is to describe the mysteries of existence, surely he would do better by leaving himself free to choose whatever analogies best fitted any one mystery. And it must be admitted that there is truth in this contention: systematic metaphysics must sacrifice something in the matter of appropriateness to any one given mystery. But anything the description of each mystery thus loses in appropriateness it more than makes up in what we may call a fullness of analogical overtones. For the peculiar quality of each mystery will be so expressed as to relate it to the whole system of other mysteries: the common analogical convention is a common measure which relates each to all. The Aristotelian system is, once more, an admirable example of this. It provides a common metaphysical grammar in which everything in heaven and earth can be more or less adequately expressed. To express anything in this grammar is immediately to feel its due relation to everything else that we have hitherto expressed in it. It is this fact which chiefly explains the sway still exercised over theological minds by the Aristotelian system; even now, when it is cut off from the logical and physical roots from which it grew. Logic and physics move on and use other conventions, but the theologian is tempted still to use the Aristotelian metaphysical language, because he above all other men has an interest in seeing all the mysteries of existence in their relation to a single unity. And since the break-up of the Aristotelian-Christian system at the Renaissance, no one has had the genius to construct so variable, so supple, so extensible and consistent a metaphysical language.

Let it be granted, then, that nothing properly to be called metaphysics appears until we have system and comprehensiveness. Yet, if we are not to be simply the slaves of a system, if we are to be able to criticize and reform it, or even to remind ourselves that reality is something more various and vital than the system can express, then we must step outside the conventions of the system and have recourse to free existential description, that is, to the description of each mystery in any analogical terms which may appear expressive. Free existential description is really prior to metaphysical system, it is the soil out of which it grows: and it is for the health of systematic metaphysics that there should always be minds in revolt against what they esteem its sterile dogmatism, and devoted to the free play of uncontrolled existential description.

Metaphysics undertakes the whole complex of natural mysteries, free existential description takes them piecemeal, and the use the two methods make of analogy differs according to their aim and scope: but both use analogy, and in essentially the same way, that is, descriptively and critically. It does not concern us here to pursue the distinction between them, but rather to exhibit their common form: and for the appreciation of this, the examination of free existential description is perhaps more immediately illuminating.

Let us now recall the question which led us into this perfunctory sketch of metaphysical procedure. What was puzzling us was the function of images in revealed truth. The scandal appeared to be, that we cannot point away from the revealed images to any imageless or 'straight' truth which the images signify. So we decided to consider the use of images outside the special province of revealed truth, and took up the broader province of metaphysics. Well, and what have we discovered? Can the metaphysician point away from the analogical statements he uses to a non-analogical truth which they state? We cannot answer yes or no to that: the question is ambiguous: the reply depends on what you mean by the non-analogical *truth*. If by 'truth' you mean a piece of true *thinking*, the answer is No: the metaphysician cannot point away from his analogically-expressed thoughts about the natural mysteries to some non-analogical thoughts about them, which mean all that the analogical thoughts mean. He has not got any such non-analogical thoughts: analogy is the proper form of metaphysical thought, in the realm of *thought* there is no getting behind it.

If, on the other hand, by 'truth' you mean the existent reality which the metaphysician is talking about, then indeed he can in a sense point to a truth outside his analogical statements, which they are designed to state. For he can point to the natural mysteries. Without analogizing he can do no more than point to them, or at the most name them: he cannot express or describe them. He can, without analogizing, say 'There is what I call myself, and there is what I call my body, and the two have something to do with one another'. But what it is they have to do with one another can only be stated in analogies. The relation of self and body is *there* in our act of existing, and it is that to which our analogical discourse reacts: but it does not get *expressed* in any parallel and non-analogical reaction.

Is this fact of irreducible analogizing so odd after all? It appears to be a simple consequence from the most obvious characteristic of all thinking whatsoever. Thinking is mental discourse, and no act of discourse can be performed without at least two terms. The sentence, not the single word, is the proper expression of thinking. A single word may express a thought, but only because further terms are taken as understood. If we say MURDER, we either mean 'Murder is going on here' or 'What so-and-so committed was nothing less than murder', or 'Murder so-and-so' or, if we are bloodthirsty enough, 'Murder away, never mind whom'.

All thinking, then, is a movement, passing, as it were, from term to term. The relation stated between term and term may be any conceivable relation: spatial collocation, temporal succession, effect and cause. But suppose we do not want to relate anything to anything else; suppose we want to consider its *nature*: for that is the proper business of the metaphysician. Certainly he deals with relations, but of them too he enquires what their *natures* are. How can we simply consider the *nature* of anything, if considering means passing from something to something else? The ordinary form of speech informs us how we can do it: we do not ordinarily ask 'What is its nature?' but 'What is it like?' To describe a thing is to compare it with other things. So, then, we express the nature of a thing by assigning it its place among the comparable natures of other things.

In comparing one thing with others, in saying what it is like, we can either use straight classification, or we cannot. Fido is like Toby, for both are dogs. Dogs are like cats, for both are mammals. But metaphysical discourse does not deal with the classifiable: the 'natural mysteries' it attempts to describe are each unique, or anyhow it is what is unique in them that it attempts to describe: and here classification lends no aid. I suppose we can say, if we like, 'the relation of person to body is like the relation of captain to boat, for both are relations', but if we do say this, we shall not be thought to have contributed much to metaphysical discussion. No: we cannot classify, and so we are condemned to sheer irreducible analogy, the attempt, never really possible, to express one thing in terms of another thing which it somehow resembles, but from which it is nevertheless diverse throughout. We try to understand the correspondence (so called) of thought to thing in terms of the correspondence to a thing shewn by its replica: but there is no point of absolutely identical form in the two relations, except what is purely trivial and metaphysically quite uninformative, e.g. that each is a two-term relation, or that in each pair the second term (thought or replica) comes into existence with a view to the first.

In order to understand, then, why metaphysics is irreducibly analogical, we need only to recognize (i) that thought requires plurality of terms (ii) that metaphysical thought attempts the expression of the unique.

We will return to the comparison between the function of metaphysical analogy and the function of revealed images. We can see at a glance how far more favourably placed the metaphysician is than the scriptural theologian. Neither of these men, it is true, can get behind the imaged form of statement, but the metaphysician's object of study is absolutely given to him in his own existence and in its environing conditions: it is about these things that his analogical statements are made, and he has such an awareness of the realities he describes as to be able to feel the relative adequacy of different analogies to them. Not so the scriptural theologian. He has got *something*, indeed, of given reality to which some of his statements refer, that is to say, the work of grace in his own soul. But not even with regard to this is he in the same position as the metaphysician. For the work of grace in one's own soul, taken as something simply given, and apart from the transcendent realities to which it is believed to be related, is not even recognizable as the work of grace. So the theologian cannot simply feel the adequacy or inadequacy of the revealed images to the object they describe: for he has not that object. He cannot criticize the revealed images from his acquaintance with their object: he can only confront them with one another.

We have not room in this lecture to take the next step forward, and follow the fortunes of imaged discourse out of metaphysics into rational theology; so we will turn aside from chasing the images, and conclude with a brief digression on the spiritual importance of metaphysical thinking itself.

Obviously (to begin with) the healthy-minded man does not need to be a metaphysician, any more than the believing Christian needs to be a theologian. The believing Christian does the sort of thinking which the theologian criticizes and regulates, and the healthy mind does the sort of thinking which the metaphysician criticizes and regulates. Since men, or anyhow some men, are speculative animals, there will always be theology as long as there is religious thinking, and in the same way there will always be metaphysics while there is ordinary healthy thinking about our natural existence. When theology is exploded, it is because the validity of religious thinking is denied: and the vindication of religious thinking then becomes the business of theology. And where metaphysics is repudiated (as it now is) it is because the ordinary healthy thinking which metaphysics criticizes is denied validity. And this is a very serious state of affairs.

What, then, is the ordinary healthy thinking of which metaphysics is the systematic elaboration? It is just contemplative thinking. Whenever the mind contemplates the deep mystery of what it is to know or to love, or to be an embodied spirit, or to be subject to the form of time, and yet able to rise above the temporal stream and to survey it: whenever we consider the vitality and the richness, the inexhaustible individuality of the being whom as wife or friend we love: when we aspire to ask of the forces of nature, not how they work simply, but what in themselves they are: when we advance from curiosity to admiration, and stand upon the brink of awe: then we are thinking in the form from which metaphysical philosophy arises.

It is useless to say, 'We can contemplate indeed, but we cannot metaphysicize'. For either our contemplation holds something real in view, or else it is a mere sensuous enjoyment, or a mere emotional attitude. If contemplation attends to what is real, then the nature of that real must be the most serious subject of intellectual enquiry: to deny this is to deny that we can think in a serious or rigorous way at all about what meets us as most real in all our experience. It is an ancient axiom that the perfection of intellect is to grasp what is: and it should be fairly evident that if we recede from this position

77

we make all serious religious belief impossible, for when we know God we know him on whom the reality of things is founded. If we surrender metaphysical enquiry, we shall vainly invoke supernatural revelation to make up for our metaphysical loss of nerve. For if our cravenheartedness surrenders the ground of metaphysics, it will have surrendered the bridgehead which the supernatural liberator might land upon. Get a man to see the mysterious depth and seriousness of the act by which he and his neighbour exist, and he will have his eyes turned upon the bush in which the supernatural fire appears, and presently he will be prostrating himself with Moses, before him who thus names himself: 'I am that I am'.

To reject metaphysics is equivalent to saying that there are no serious questions for the human mind except those which fall under the special sciences. We can ask historically why the crucifixion of Christ came about: physiologically, whether he died of heart-failure or by some other cause: psychologically, what train of thoughts and feeling induced him to put his neck into the noose: morally, how his action squared with a copy-book of ethical imperatives. But we cannot consider what in itself, in its intensity and elevation of being, in its divinity, the voluntary passion of Christ was. We have a first interest in keeping this road unblocked, the road by which a serious and realistic wonder advances through the contemplation of Christ's manhood into the adoration of his deity, that it may lay hold upon the Eternal Son, who, hanging on the Cross, is enthroned in Heaven; who, lying in the sepulchre, lies in the bosom of the Father; and standing in the upper room, breathes forth from the heart of all being the Paraclete, the Holy Ghost. *Now therefore to the indivisible Trinity and social Unity, one Godhead in three Persons, be ascribed as is most justly due all might, dominion, majesty and power, henceforth and for ever.*

V

*The Heavens declare the Glory of God, and the firma-
ment sheweth his handiwork. There is no speech nor
language, neither are their voices heard among them.
Their sound is gone forth into all the earth, and their
words to the end of the world.* PSALM XIX. 1-4

The heavens declare the glory of God, their voiceless
words sound in the ear of an attentive reason; so a natural
knowledge of God is acquired from his handiwork. We have
now to consider this natural knowledge of God from a particular point of view—we have to describe the part played in it
by images. After that we will look at the even more mysterious part which images play in the supernatural and revealed
knowledge of God.

In the last lecture we prepared the ground for the enquiry
we have now to undertake. For, seeing that God's existence
is one of the topics of metaphysics, we spoke generally of
metaphysical method. Now we must narrow the field, we
must isolate the question of God's existence from all other
metaphysical questions, and study it by itself.

The first thing to be explained is that God's existence is one
of the mysteries of metaphysics, not one of the puzzles of
metaphysics. Let me explain what I mean by the distinction
between mysteries and puzzles. The metaphysician studies
mysteries, mysteries of our natural existence, which are
simply there in any case, whether we metaphysicize about
them or not. We simply have a personal identity, for example, and we simply have a physical body; but the nature of
these two realities, still more of the relation between them, is
highly mysterious. Such mysteries the metaphysician wrestles

79

with; he attempts to describe them by means of analogies. In his attempt to describe, puzzles are certain to arise—puzzles interior to the particular analogical description he chooses to employ. Since no analogy ever fits perfectly, the adaptation of any analogical description to the object described must create puzzles. How is the description to be made either consistent or suitable? For example, the Aristotelians took in hand to describe the mystery of the knowing act. Under the descriptive conventions proper to their system, they found it necessary to distinguish between the active and the receptive powers of the intellect. When they had done this, the puzzle arose, how the active intellect and the receptive intellect were to be related to one another in one mind. This is a puzzle of the Aristotelian system; it is not a mystery of existence. We can be rid of the puzzle at a single stroke by refusing to be Aristotelians. If we do not choose to use their conventions or talk their language, the puzzle is no puzzle for us. But the mystery of existence remains. We may not wish to talk about the mysterious character of the knowing act in Aristotelian terms, but the mystery of the knowing act is still with us. We may adopt a convention of speech which makes it impossible for us to talk about the mystery of knowledge—that is quite easy: I dare say the Hottentot language would save us from discourse upon this and other metaphysical mysteries. But the mysteries do not vanish because we talk Hottentot, and they will catch us out one of these days, constraining us to speak of them in some language which will allow them to get a foothold in our minds.

The believer in God must suppose that the mystery of God's existence is no mere puzzle, but a genuine mystery, presented to us by the stuff of our own existence: whether we describe it well or ill, whether we speak of it or ignore it, it is still there. For God appears in our thoughts as the name of a real being we attempt to describe, not as a convenient analogical term used by us in describing something else, in describing the moral conscience, for example. We cannot abolish every question in which the name of God occurs at a single stroke, simply by refusing to talk the special language of this or that philosophical system. 'God' is not a factitious term, like Aristotle's 'active intellect'. So believing philosophers say: not so the unbelieving philosophers; in fact, this is the very point where we part company with them. We say to them: 'Though you reject one description of transcendent being, you still have the mystery of transcendence on your hands to describe.' They say to us: 'There is no mystery of transcendence. There is, in the working out of certain metaphysical systems, the puzzle of transcendence. We take no interest in those systems, nor in that puzzle.'

Now the most serious philosophical task that I could undertake would be to go on with the debate from this point. It is the business of believing philosophers to show reason why God's existence is a genuine mystery, not a factitious puzzle. I cannot undertake so momentous a task here, nor is it the business we have in hand. Meanwhile, just to keep our courage up, let us observe that the mystery of transcendence is not got rid of at a stroke by the resolution to talk a language which ignores it. Like nature, it keeps on turning up: *expellas furca, tamen usque recurret.* Rationalism must exorcise it again and again with bell, book and Bunsen burner: and then there it is, haunting us once more. Please do not think that I consider this a decisive consideration: there are some superstitions which die extremely hard; theological belief might be one of those.

Believing and unbelieving philosophers differ as to whether the mystery about God's existence is a mystery at all. Is not this something of a scandal to start with? One might think that philosophers would disagree in their *descriptions* of the natural mysteries, but would at least agree as to which the natural mysteries are. There may be a scandal here: but if so, it is not a scandal peculiar to the question about God's existence. There is a disagreement about other natural mysteries also, as to whether they are genuine mysteries or not. To many of us human free-will appears the most pressing and unescapable of natural mysteries; yet some people think it to be a factitious puzzle; and there is a sect of people who allow there to be no natural mysteries at all.

To accept the mystery about God's existence as a genuine mystery may be to beg the chief of all metaphysical questions. Nevertheless, since we are here speaking from within our Christian faith, let us beg it, and advance to a fresh point. Supposing that the mystery about God is somehow just *there*, let us ask in what way it forces itself upon our attention.

If I were asked in general how the natural mysteries present themselves to the metaphysician's attention, I should be inclined to make a simple classification of them into two groups, 'me' and 'not me'. Some natural mysteries are parts of the form of my own active existence—my free-will, for example, or my embodied state. These are the 'me' group, and I become aware of them in attending to my own action. The 'not me' group are presented by the environment with which I interact: I become aware of them in attending not to my own action in itself, but to the field in which it plays. Such mysteries are: the nature of merely physical bodies, or the relation of other finite minds to mine. Into which of these classes shall we try to put the mystery of God? Hardly into the 'me' class—God cannot be the form of my existence, surely; still less can he be one part or detail of the form of my existence. It seems more hopeful to try to put the mystery of God into the group of mysteries that are not me: unless, that is, I have decided to be a pantheist.

Let us consider, then, the way in which the realities that are not me shew to me their mysterious existence. On the level of common-sense, of course, we take physical bodies and other people's minds for granted: we take it that they are simply there. But presently some of the well-known puzzles of philosophy perplex us, and we begin to wonder whether the beings which compose our environment are what we had taken them to be. Our first reaction to this doubt is to say: 'Well,

there is *something* out there, and it is really impinging on me
with causal force But perhaps my mind and my senses have
been wrongly interpreting the nature of this mysterious
energy which plays upon me from without.' I may assist my
imagination by using the figure of a spider's web, of which
the threads are lines of physical relation. The centre, where all
the threads run together, is the focal point of my existence.
But it would be the focus of nothing, unless the threads of
relation ran in all directions towards other centres of being.
At any moment any of the threads may be pulled, and it may
be pulled from either end. It is pulled from the centre of the
web, when an action of mine has an effect on somebody or
something else: it is pulled from the circumference, when
somebody or something else so acts as to have an effect on
me. It is out of the pulling of the thread, we think, that our
exterior knowledge arises. Our senses directly react to the
trembling of the thread: on the basis of it, they give us sensual
signs of that other something or somebody, and on those signs
we found an immediate intellectual supposition of that other's
existence. If, then, the suggestion comes to me that my suppositions about that other are inadequate and bewildering,
that its real being is a mystery, my first reaction is this. 'Anyhow,' I say, 'there is the fact of active relation. There is the
spider's web, and the threads really tremble, they are really
attached at their outer ends: their tremors express something
that really happens at their outer termini. It may be, however,
that my senses and intellect combined give a highly mythical
account of the real activities out there to which the tremors
of the threads respond.' I do not say that such a line of
reflection is very profound: I simply say that it is how my
thoughts immediately arrange themselves, when the suggestion is made to me that my knowledge of finite beings is a
mystery.

I observe something further. I observe that if it is suggested
to me that my knowledge of God is a mystery, I am inclined
to transfer my account of the mystery of finite knowledge to

the mystery of knowing the infinite. I say 'Yes, indeed: God must be all unlike what I suppose him to be. But anyhow, I may believe that my suppositions about him arise out of my active relation to him. That at least may be solid fact. There is the thread of my relation to him trembling with his action upon me: from that tremor my mind, by whatever secret and baffling processes, makes her conjecture of God.'

This is what I all too readily suppose. Further reflection shows that it will not do: my relation with God is not an environmental disturbance on which a particular act of my consciousness can be based. My existence does not *come under* God's causal influence, so that I may be aware of the shock. To his causality my existence itself is due. A shock is administered to me by my being flung into water, but no shock is administered to me by my being flung into existence, for to feel the plunge into water I must be there before I plunge, but before I am plunged into existence I *am not*. According to the Freudians, we can in a dim manner experience being born, but not even the most precocious of us can experience being conceived, still less can we experience being created: and it makes no difference to this conclusion, that whereas our conception was an event in the past, our creation continuously and timelessly underlies our being. It remains that we are there to act and suffer simply in so far as our creation takes effect. We do not therefore suffer it, or react to it. Our relation to our Creator is real enough, but what arises on the basis of it is not a particular state or act of our conscious existence, but our whole conscious existence.

When I think of myself in active relation to environmental energies I take both my existence and their existence for granted, and ask what I do to them, or they to me. If I try to think myself in active relation to God, I do the same thing. I take my existence as well as his existence for granted, and then ask, perhaps not what I do to him, but anyhow, what he does to me. But the answer is 'nothing'. Once I have taken my existence for granted, I can find nothing that my Creator does to me. What he does to me is to cause my existence; but I was not there to experience that, I can only exercise experience once I am created.

The process of my creation is neither an action nor a passion of my existence. Not an action, for I can do nothing about it; nor a passion, for I am not there to undergo it. It is simply the act of God's existence. It has not two focuses, one in God and one in me: its focus is simply in God. I cannot first be aware of my creation as something impinging on my focus, and then proceed to interpret it as something arising from God's focus. If I am aware of it at all, I must be aware of it in him from the start. I must be simply aware of the divine or infinite act which is God himself—not, certainly, of God in all the aspects of his infinite active being, but God in that aspect of his action which looks towards my creation.

But this, it may be objected, cannot be true and is not true. I am not aware of God's creative act unmediated. I am only aware of it, in so far as it is mediated to me by my own created existence, or by some other created existence. Yes: but to say that, is not to determine the nature of the mediation which the created existence supplies. We have so far only dismissed the suggestion that the creature mediates knowledge of the creator by undergoing his creative influence. It may mediate knowledge of him in other ways, for example, by offering material for a shadow or image of him. Somewhat as though my eyes and my hands were by some necessity wholly employed in a field of finite relationships outspread in front of me, so that I was unable to have direct awareness of a current of creative power which continually sustained and supplied me from behind. Yet the vast shadow of my Creator himself might fall over my shoulder into the field of finite things before my eyes. Then the visibility of the shadow to me would depend on the substance it found on which to print its figure. A shadow may fall for ever imperceptible through empty air, but even mist or smoke on the motes in the sunbeam will embody it, better still a solid surface, a shining surface best of all. So perhaps our awareness of the infinite Act depends on the materials for a shadow of him presented by finite existence: perhaps that sheerly given metaphysical mystery with which rational theology wrestles is the shadow of the Infinite in finite being.

All this, as you will be quick to point out, is pure metaphor, unworthy to find a place in philosophical discourse. True, but metaphors are sometimes the dawning of intelligence: whether they are or are not we do not know, until we have decoded them. Let us see what we can do with this figure of the shadow.

The problem of our knowing God, we will say, is never a problem of his being made present, but always of our being able to apprehend his presence. A star in the Milky Way needs to be made present to me by the passage of light from it to me; if it is small enough and distant enough it may be impotent to achieve effective presence with me. As between God and me, this sort of question does not arise. True, the *mode* of his presence to me is as yet a mystery: it is not, for example, by way of particular and variable causal influence. But if we are prepared to consider the possibility of his being known at all, we may simply concede his presence, in whatever fashion. The problem will be, not about his presence to our minds, but about our minds' receptivity for him. Will he pass through us completely, as perpendicular light through a pane of perfect glass, or, to change the metaphor, will he find nothing to illuminate in us, like a ray passing into a hollow sphere lined with velvet black?

Our minds, in fact, are neither mirrors nor containers: their receptivity depends on what they can *do*, on their ability to busy themselves with their object, to express it in discoursing on it. But it seems that our minds are impotent to discourse on God, to express God. No doubt once we have obtained knowledge of him, we may assign to the object of our knowledge a name coined for the purpose, for example, the name 'God' itself. But that is after the event; our ability now to use the name 'God' significantly casts no light on the act of discourse by which we first made God's idea a part of our mental existence.

Let us consider our predicament. We can only know God in expressing God: and we can express him in no other terms than such as are already significant to us, terms we already have in familiar use. Such terms will be terms descriptive of finite existence, for hitherto we are supposed to know no other existence. Therefore our power of knowing God will depend upon the resources of our finite experience. Only in proportion as our experience of finite existence affords analogies in terms of which God can be discoursed upon, shall we be able, in discoursing on God, to actualize an apprehension of God: for without discourse there is no intellectual apprehension.

From such a statement as this we may readily form the picture of Nature presenting to the human mind a colour-box of analogies, and saying to her, 'Here are your colours: now go ahead, and paint the portrait. Take a touch of spirituality from human virtue, a touch of sublime changelessness from the mountains, a tint of bright ubiquity from the light, and paint the image of God.' 'Ah,' our mind would have to reply, 'but unhappily I cannot see the subject I am trying to paint. It was only in painting that I was to see him, and until I have painted I do not know how to begin, how to lay the colours, or indeed what colours to choose.'

What is the way out of this *impasse*? There is no way out of it, because it is not really an *impasse* at all. For the same situation confronts us in all knowledge, and not only in the knowledge of God. It is always absurd to ask how the human mind can voluntarily set about thinking of something, the like of which it never thought about before. All our voluntary thinking is ultimately the development of involuntary thinking which has already occurred in us. How do our first thoughts about ordinary physical things arise? Are they not part and parcel of the involuntary process of sense-perception? It is

87

only by the refinement and development of these involuntary thoughts that we can think *at will* of physical nature. In the same way our first thoughts about ourselves are part and parcel of our conscious behaviour; and we begin to behave before we choose to behave. We first find ourselves behaving, and only at a second stage reflect at will upon ourselves as the subjects of the behaviour. By this analogy we might expect that our first thoughts about God must be involuntary, too: only when we had begun to think about God could we elaborate and refine at will our mental picture of God.

But what should make us begin to think about God in an involuntary way? As a drowned man breathes by being dragged through the motions of breathing, so our thought about *physical* things begins by our being dragged through the acts of physical thinking: the dragging being done by brute sensation. So too in the case of thought about self: we are dragged through the first motions of it by our animal behaviour. But what is to drag us through the first motions of thought about God? Nothing simply happens to us in this connexion: we do not suddenly perceive God through the senses without, we do not find him suddenly functioning as a factor of our existence within. God is perceived neither by the sense-bound acts of mind, nor by the mental acts which are tied to behaviour. Is he then perceived by the simple mind? But the simple mind has no organ for perceiving anything, unless we allow the name of 'organ' to her act of discoursing about a thing. If the mind begins to perceive God involuntarily, it must be that acts of discourse about God are forced upon the mind.

But what can force upon the mind an act of discourse about God? Nothing, presumably, unless it be an experience of finite existence. Again, how can elements of finite existence force a discourse about God upon the mind which experiences them? Only in one way that I can conceive: in getting themselves taken by the mind as an embodied discourse about

God, as symbols or shadows of God. If, for example, I were
to be meditating upon my own acts of knowledge and will,
knowledge which is never a tenth part adequate to the real
nature of anything existing, will which is always nine parts
bound; and if I were suddenly to find myself taking them as
reduced or confused or adulterated instances of sheer will
and knowledge, things in their essence perfect and absolute:
then my own existence would have presented to my thinking
mind the shadow of absolute spirit, which is the shadow of
God.

Before we go on with our proper business, which is to
consider the shadow of God in finite being, we must pause to
explain ourselves about one of the phrases we have used.
Finite objects of experience, we have said, *force* the mind to
take them as shadows of absolute being, or *drag* the mind
through the motions of thinking the absolute in thinking of
them. This, surely, is nonsense. How can the objects of finite
experience exercise such a compulsion on the mind? We will
agree immediately that *dragging* or *compelling* are, in such an
application, very violent metaphors: their merit is simply to
emphasize the difference between voluntary thinking such as
that done by a philosopher thinking out his natural theology,
and involuntary thinking, such as happens to him when he
finds himself instinctively taking his own spiritual acts as
finite, that is, as limited instances of something intrinsically
infinite. But it is not really proper to talk about involuntary
thinking on any level as happening under exterior compulsion. To take sense perception, for example. It is proper, no
doubt, to think of the mind as being abundantly active
throughout the process: the mind is, as it were, out for
experience, and in co-operating with sensation follows its
own bent and exercises its own energy. It is not forced or
dragged by sensation, it exploits the occasion which sensation
offers. But in exploiting it, it acts by nature rather than by
choice: in fact it acts like the digestion. Digestion seizes and
assimilates any suitable matter, of its own vital motion indeed,

but not by deliberate choice: if the suitable matter is given to it, the digestive process simply does act. So with involuntary thinking: the mind simply does act when the sensation gives it the occasion: it does not choose whether it will or no.

So the mind which first takes some finite object as a shadow of the infinite, acts involuntarily in the sense that it acts by nature, not by choice. The mind must be thought of as placed between two presences: the simple presence of the infinite, and the changing and various presence of the finite. It has a natural tendency to become aware of both presences: but it cannot become aware of the infinite except by symbolizing it in terms of the finite. When finite objects happen to have been brought into such a mental focus that they are capable of acting as symbols of the infinite, then the mind's power to know the infinite leaps into actualization, seeing the finite in the infinite, and the infinite in the finite.

The event that we are speaking of is a double event: two things are happening. First, there is an ordinary pedestrian act of the mind, appreciating some aspect of finite existence. Second, there is a sublimer act, by which the finite object is itself appreciated as a symbol of the infinite. Of these two acts, the former and more pedestrian is unambiguously directed towards a finite object: the second and sublimer act is ambiguous in its direction; it bears both on a finite and on an infinite object, for it treats the one as a symbol of the other, and so seems to hang between earth and heaven. This being so, we shall naturally expect the first act to exercise an attraction upon the second and pull it in the earthwards direction.

Let me explain what I mean by this perhaps not very well-chosen language. What we are talking about is an act of mind in which something finite serves as a symbol for the infinite. The mind which performs such an act will be bound to tip in one of two directions: it cannot hold the balance even. Either it will take itself to be thinking about the infinite being, or it will take itself to be thinking about the finite being. Suppose, for example, my own act of knowledge or will is the finite symbol to be employed. Then one of two things will happen: either I shall be saying, 'God's existence is the absolute expression of such knowledge and will as these of mine': or I shall be saying, 'This knowledge and this will of mine are but limited, cramped, adulterated expressions of sheer knowledge and sheer will, activities intrinsically infinite and divine.' In the first case I shall be thinking of God by the light of myself: in the second case I shall be thinking of myself as a partial ray which falls from the full brightness of God.

There is nothing to choose between these two forms of the symbolizing act so long as we think of that act apart from any particular context. But, in the present argument, we have got a particular context for it. We are not thinking of any men at any time symbolizing the infinite in terms of the finite. We are thinking of the special case of a man who, for the first time, takes a finite thing as a symbol of the infinite in the process of thinking about the finite thing. Now this man, by hypothesis, is thinking about the finite, not about the infinite, when the sudden and mysterious act of symbolization takes place. It is fairly certain, then, that this man's act of symbolization will take the form of a thinking about the finite under the light of the infinite, not a thinking about the infinite through its expression in the finite. He will see himself as thinking primarily about the natural object, not about God. The natural mystery which is the starting-point of rational theology is the finite manifesting itself as the shadow of the infinite.

As Descartes pointed out, once we have arrived at a certain level of conceptual clarification, it makes no odds which way round the act of symbolization takes shape. The intelligent appreciation of the finite as finite involves the appreciation of infinity, and it matters not the least on which of the two our attention is first focussed, we shall shift it to the other directly. But this is only so when a certain conceptual clarification of the mystery has been achieved or accepted. At an earlier, more inchoate stage it is of course of huge practical importance that what we are labouring with appears to be located in the finite, not in the infinite. To the theistic philosopher it seems that people are everywhere wrestling with the mystery of the shadow of the infinite, but that they have often no notion that the shadow of the infinite is what they are wrestling with: their knowledge of God therefore remains purely implicit and they are unable to bring it into explicit consciousness.

I shall now swing the argument still further in the direction in which it has been moving. We have so far talked as though the mind's real concern throughout were to know God in terms of the creature, not the creature in relation to God. We have thought of the mind as being in the presence of God always, but unable to see him until she finds a mirror in created existence which will in some measure reflect his image. We do not normally contemplate reflections in mirrors for the purpose of obtaining information about the properties of looking-glass: we look at them for knowledge of the face reflected there. On such an analogy we should suppose that the mind's vision of the shadow of God in the creature was solely for the sake of the knowledge of God. But such a suggestion is false. God alone is primal being, and the relation of any other being to him cannot be left out of account, if we are to know that other being fully. Thus the fact that my own existence is a limited and fragmentary shadow of divine existence is just as important a truth about me as about God. In one sense it casts more light on my existence, in another sense, more on God's existence. If we consider that I know nothing at all of God's existence except through his finite image in my existence, then it may seem that more light is cast by that image on his existence than on mine; for I do at least know that I exist without observing God's image in me, but I do not even know that God exists without observing his image in me. On the other hand, if our test is adequacy to the nature of the object known, we must say that more light is cast on my existence than on God's: for my being a fragmentary finite image of him is an infinitely poor clue to his infinite being, whereas the fact that, being what I am, I am a finite shadow of the infinite reality, is a tolerably good clue to my metaphysical status.

By this line of argument we work our way back to a formula which we used some while ago—natural knowledge of God is primarily the knowledge of existence at our own level, including the knowledge that it is existence of a secondary or dependent kind. For in such a knowledge of our own existence there is some knowledge of God involved. It is because God's infinity is shadowed forth in finite existence that the knowledge of God as absolute being is natural knowledge to a finite mind, in the sense in which we have defined natural knowledge.

Let us, by way of conclusion, collect an answer to the question with which this lecture began: what is the function of images in the natural knowledge of God? The natural theologian is a metaphysician, and the metaphysician, as we have seen, is condemned to use analogical or imaged statement in any case: but the metaphysician has the compensation that the natural mystery he strives to describe is actually present in his own existence, so that he *feels* the applicability or inapplicability of his proposed analogies to the object they should express. Is the rational theologian simply a case of the metaphysician, or is there something peculiar about his predicament?

There is certainly something peculiar about his predicament, because there is something singular about his object. God's creative act is present to us in so singular a manner that we do not know whether to say that it is present or absent. In the case of other mysteries we can at least name them without analogizing: for example, we have seen that I can say, 'There is my moral person and there is my body, and the two have something to do with one another.' It is only when we go on to describe this something that we must analogize. But in the case of knowing God we cannot name him until an analogical act of mind has taken place: it is only in being aware of something finite as an analogy of God that we begin to be aware of God at all.

From this extraordinary conclusion we might be tempted to infer the corollary that the analogy used in rational theology functions in the same way as the image used to convey revealed truth: for neither in revelation nor in rational theology can we point away from the image to that which the image signifies: in both we must be content to refer to the reality by understanding what the image tells us. Nevertheless, rational analogies and revealed images concerning God do not function in the same way: and we can express the difference by saying that the rational analogies are *natural* images: the revealed figures are not, in the sense intended, *natural*.

The rational analogies are natural, first of all, in the sense that they may be, and originally are, spontaneous: unless finite things put themselves upon us as symbols of deity we can have no natural knowledge of God. Revealed images do not do this: they are authoritatively communicated. The stars may seem to speak of a maker, the moral sense of a law-giver: but there is no pattern of being we simply meet, which speaks of Trinity in the Godhead or the efficacy of the Sacraments. Many symbols, indeed, suggest the Trinity and the Sacraments to a Christian, but they are the product of faith already accorded to a revelation already received: they are not just there, like moral reason or the Milky Way.

Rational analogies are natural in a second sense: the analogy which the natural symbol appears to bear to God is founded on a real relation in which it stands towards God. Suppose, for example, I take my will as a symbol of God, because it seems to be a limited instance of something intrinsically infinite, sheer creativity. In such a case the symbolical relation corresponds with a real relation: in making me a voluntary being God has made me to participate in his own creative energy; my will symbolizes God because it participates of God. Whereas revealed images are commonly just parables. For example, I am taught the mystery of Christ's mystical body in terms of physical organism. But there is no real and causal relation between natural organisms and Christ's mystical body: bodies, by being bodies, do not really participate in the mystery of saving incorporation. I do in fact participate in Christ's mystical body, but not by being a natural bodily creature: I participate in Christ's body by a supernatural and imperceptible gift; and this gift is no part of the figure by which revelation teaches me about the body of Christ. On the contrary, I need the revealed figures just as much to teach me about my supernatural gift as I need them to teach me about the divine body in which, by reason of the gift, I partake. Only the figures are revealed, and the figures are simply parables. Let us quote St. Paul. 'As the body is one, and has many organs, yet all the organs of the body, being many, are one body, so is Christ.'

Rational analogies are, by contrast, natural, but in being natural they come no nearer to being adequate. They speak of a God everywhere immediately present, but everywhere deeply incomprehensible, no less in the manner of his presence, than in the nature of his existence. May he who is so near to our being and so far from our conceiving forgive our belittling speech concerning his inviolable majesty, and assist us rather to praise, in words he has himself revealed, the One God in three Persons, Father, Son and Holy Ghost: *to whom be therefore ascribed as is most justly due all might, dominion, majesty and power, henceforth and for ever.*

VI

We cannot but be interested in what is most near and most real to us: and if I have hitherto dwelt disproportionately upon the natural knowledge of God, it will be because of its place in my mind. I know there are those who can readily enter into the apprehension of divine mysteries by the direct road of revealed Truth; and to such men it often seems that all the labour of the philosophers to establish a natural knowledge of God is a vain endeavour, since believers have no use for it, and unbelievers cannot be constrained to acknowledge it. But have not the believers a use for it? Those are happy, no doubt, who can enter directly into the promised land of Christ by the invocation of his Name. But such·will not wish to forget that there are others, men who often find it best to climb the ladder from the bottom, proceeding through the natural to the supernatural knowledge of God. Are those Christian minds really so rare whose nearest gate into the invisible world is a simple awe at natural fact? I need but to consider that I am able from moment to moment to draw my breath; to live by an act which is my very being, yet is not mine, for I do not breathe by choice or will, still less by my own devising; and then to consider what is more fully mine, my act of thought, an act which aspires to identify itself with the objective truth of things, to see all beings, and myself among them, impartially, as though from a great height, as though from the steps of a heavenly throne: my thought which is nevertheless momentary, precariously seated in a tremor of my cerebral nerves, and embodied in the trifling act of stringing together words, or the imaged ghosts of

96

words; when I see how much of being and of truth is some-how balanced on the absurd pin-point of my perishable moment, I step into the contemplation of him who does not alter or pass, who possesses and masters all he is or knows.

These thoughts are real to us: from the simple appreciation of our finitude we pass to the consideration of the infinite Being. And afterwards, in a reflective hour, we wish to know by what process our thought has moved, and in what sense we can ascribe validity to it: and we call this enquiry rational theology, the enquiry into man's natural knowledge of God.

But is it the enquiry into *man's* natural knowledge of God, or merely into ours? Can we reasonably take the spontaneous reflections of modern men, of Christians, even of would-be philosophers, as typical of those original apprehensions by which man has seen the shadow of God in nature? No, we cannot take them as typical; but we are bound to take them as standard. There are certain fields in which the typical gets us nowhere, and we always do think by standards. No one thinks of virtue or excellence of any sort in terms of Gallup polls. All species of mammals are equally mammalian, but not all wise men are equally wise: we are bound to think of wisdom proper as a true or perfect wisdom, and men as wise in so far as they approach to it. Now natural religion seems to be a sort of wisdom. No doubt an uninstructed Hottentot can be as *religious* as a Christian philosopher, in the sense of being as whole-hearted about the religion he has. But his religion is not so high a wisdom, and we only call his beliefs beliefs about *God* in so far as they approximate to some standard theistic belief. And what is our standard belief? It must be what we believe ourselves: it is nonsense to pretend to believe and at the same time to pretend that a belief other than our own is our standard of what should be believed. Some students of the religious history of mankind, for certain limited purposes belonging to their art, have attempted to find flat-rate definitions of theistic belief, equally valid for all instances: the results are depressing. What are we to say if we

97

are to keep the Hottentot on board without crowding the Christian into the water? Shall we call the divine 'A non-natural power able to help or harm and open to conciliation by ritual practice?' One sees the Christian on his toes to dive out of the ship which sails under this device: and if you can keep him on board, it is only by exploiting the shameless ambiguity of the formula. The Christian does not mean by 'conciliating' God what the Hottentot means, nor does he mean the same by 'non-natural power', nor, to start with, has he the same ideas about what is natural and what is not.

Indeed, the search for flat-rate definitions in religion is an unprofitable exercise: and if we let our thought take its natural course, instead of making it hobble down pseudo-scientific alleys, we shall all think of 'religion' as covering the religion we believe, together with other systems of belief in so far as they approximate to that. For the moment we are discounting supernatural revelation, and considering natural religion: by which we are, therefore, bound to understand our own apprehensions of God through nature, together with those of the Gentiles, so far as they participate in or approximate to the form of our own. Men have always been apprehending the shadow of God in Nature, but in many partial aspects and under much confusion of mind: the first apprehensions were not the best: *quasi pedetemptim intravimus in cognitionem veritatis.*

The apprehension of God as infinite being and first universal cause may be the quintessence of natural religion, but it lies deeply hidden in the confused thinking of primitive men. They are little aware of the mystery of sheer creation: they are more concerned with particular manifestations of creative power, in the growth of their crops or the child-bearing of their wives. We were saying in a previous lecture that there is only one relation between the creature and the Creator, the single fact of being created: but this single relation is a channel which sometimes runs water, and sometimes runs wine—indeed, what passes through it allows of an infinite variety. We cannot ask 'Does God do nothing for us but create us?'

for in our creation all else is comprehended. God never ceases to create us, and he creates us thus or thus. Every distinct act that I perform—for example, my endeavour now to understand and to speak—rests on a distinct intention in God's creative act: everything that flows out in the stream was first in the hidden and inviolable fountain, except the mud which the current scoops up from its bed.

This being so, it is natural enough that the divine cause should be first seen in particular effects, and even thought of as a plurality of particular causes: the spirit of growth causes growth, the spirit of birth causes birth, the spirit of love causes love, and so on. And more especially God was seen as the archetype and cause of crucial human functions which were performed with difficulty. The fact that my act of trying to speak or understand reposes on God's creative intention for me does not remove the necessity of effort on my part: but that effort is made more fruitfully, I trust, and with fuller confidence if I remember the creative act on which it is founded. And so I, because it is my business, if I can, to think, must specially concern myself with the figure of God considered as archetypal wisdom.

In primitive societies in which the tradition of learning and the rule of discipline were imposed by paternal authority, the father saw himself as the representative of a divine and archetypal father, who might, in fact, be an actual or supposed human ancestor, clothed with the functions of ultimate and creative paternity. When human kings arose, invisible divine kings stood behind their thrones. Indeed, kingship worthy of the name is distinguished from mere leadership by the divinity which supports it. Now, if kings arose with divine support, we might suppose that the divine king was already known: for how can the human king be clothed with divine authority except by a divine king already acknowledged? But then, on the other hand, until men have seen human kings, how can they know what a divine king would be? In fact, the human king and his divine archetype arise at once, they are inseparable: each makes the other. *Caelo tonantem credidimus Jovem regnare: praesens divus habebitur Augustus....*

The divine King establishes human royalty: a new divine archetype stood behind prophecy. Prophecy, in its greatness, involved the endeavour to comprehend and to fulfil historical destiny. The prophet saw himself frankly as a magician, able to predict by the spirit, able also to make and destroy by the powerful breath of his word; but there stood behind him the divine prophet, the cosmic magician, whose word was of such power that its mere utterance had shaped the world out of chaos, its blessings and curses changed the destiny of nations as clay vessels are marred and made under the potter's finger. It was only by communion with the omnipotent master of spells, and in unquestioned obedience to his word, that Isaiah could preach the Assyrian host back from the defences of Jerusalem, or Jeremiah, under a more cruel obedience, could shake down the guilty walls of Zion in face of Chaldaean assault.

The kingly archetype had its origin at a time, a few thousand years before Christ: the prophetic archetype burst on the world in the recorded history of Israel. An archetype of great and still unexhausted power shone upon us in the later Renaissance, when along with the human physicist there appeared the divine physicist, the God of deism, the God of Descartes, who had imposed on the universe by a creative *fiat* that very regularity of iron law which the scientist set out to discover under God's guarantee.

The believer will surely find it an impressive fact that our family, our state, our sense for world-history, our all-conquering science, were brought to the birth under the inspiration of divine archetypes. It is testimony to the power and naturalness of religion, that men have not been able to have confidence in great developments of human function, unless they could apprehend in their working the presence and authority of God. Yet it is an equally impressive fact that the family, the state, history and science, once they have established themselves must be naturalized. Perhaps only a father with supernatural awe to clothe him could have created the civilizing patriarchal family, but a father clothed with supernatural awe is a domestic tyrant and a pillar of barbarism: the family must be humanized if civilization is to proceed. Only a king who ruled by divine right could establish a state on something wider than the ties of blood, and something less cruel than force: but kings are not, in fact, 'earthly gods' nor magical persons: political power is human, and intelligible, and politics must be rescued from stultifying hierarchy. Nothing, perhaps, but the prophets' dramatic attempt to predict and wield the destiny of peoples in the name of God could have created the sense of history as an intrinsically meaningful forward movement: but prophetism must be got rid of before scientific history can begin, for the dynamic of historical process is not rightly estimated by intuitions of a moralistic divine teleology in battles and famines.

The most interesting case for us is that which stands nearest to us, the case of physical science. Professor Collingwood, in the most paradoxical of his writings, calls on us to rally round the Athanasian Creed and save scientific civilization. His reasoning seems to me to contain two serious mistakes—first as to the connexion between Christian theology and scientific deism: second as to the connexion between scientific deism and science itself. The emergence of scientific deism was certainly conditioned, historically, by a long tradition of Christian theologizing, but scientific deism was not for all that itself a Christian phenomenon, but an expression of natural religion, emerging as the ground of a purely natural activity, viz. scientific enquiry. Then as to the second error: the connexion between deism and science was not logical, but historical and dynamic. Deism supplied the dynamism which set science afloat, but science can now proceed, like politics or history or family morals, under its own steam, and without any winds of theological magic to fill its sails. Those who prove that science cannot be irreligious in spirit by appealing to the original connexion between deism and science are making things too easy for themselves.

The reason why archetypes become dangerous is that they favour dogmatisms. The father-God archetype, understood in the patriarchal sense, attaches an absolute value to paternal discipline which it does not possess. It suggests that God acts more through a patriarchy exerted over us than, say, through any light inwardly directing us: a doctrine which is as theoretically indefensible as it is practically stultifying. And the divine archetype of scientific deism suggests that God is specially concerned with flat-rate general laws, and leads in the end to a soulless physicalism, a contempt for individuality and a denial of providence.

> The first almighty Cause
> *Acts not by partial, but by general laws,*

is, taken strictly, blasphemous nonsense. General Law has no theological privilege. The action of the finite forces of which the world is composed has an aspect of uniformity, and equally an aspect of particularity: each aspect of the creature's functioning is based on a corresponding intention in God's creative act. Indeed the only security against the false suggestions of the archetypes is the reduction of them to creative intentions. God is not intrinsically the principle of general law, he simply intends the uniformity which is proper to his creatures, along with everything else he intends for them. Nor is he intrinsically the principle of paternal authority: he simply wills that it should play that part which it has to play in the perfecting of mankind.

The reduction of the archetypes to creative intentions is only possible to us if we have a highly philosophical, some would say, a highly rarefied, conception of what God is in himself. If he is not to be tied to any of the archetypes, if he is not to be essentially this or that, he must be simply pure and infinite essence. And so a natural apprehension of God which begins by seeing him as the archetype of this or that natural function, is driven by its own practical dangers into the 'natural theology' of tradition. It must come to know God as simply that infinite creative Act which underlies all finite acts.

Let us say, then, of the archetypes that they have a purely historical justification. At a certain time in history God's creative will for man seems specially directed towards family discipline or kingly rule or scientific construction, and then his special creative intention finds a response in his creatures through the projection of the corresponding fatherly, or kingly, or 'scientific' archetype. The archetype then plays the part of a useful rhetorical exaggeration. Kingship is better supported by the doctrine that God is essentially king, than by the doctrine that kingly rule is a thing he approves and intends, a way among many ways for preserving and extending the cosmic order he creates.

We may call the archetypes just rhetorical exaggerations; but the exaggeration they employ has huge spiritual consequences. For once we see God as essentially king, father, cultivator or whatever it may be, then the human counterpart to him becomes a revelation of God, and what he achieves becomes visible and particular divine action. If Isaiah is God's prophet, his word is a divine intervention; if David is the Lord's Anointed, his victories are the hand of God; the astonished eyes of man may watch the act of naked omnipotence, when the Philistines fall before him. If we reduce the archetypes to creative intentions, then nothing in the world (it would seem) is any more a revelation of God than anything else: it is not the king, the prophet or the sage who reveals God: any finite or created being can point us to the infinite and increate; and God must be credited with a special creative intention equally in respect of every creature. God intends the man, he also intends the microbe who kills the man. But if the whole of nature and everything in it is equally sanctioned by the divine will, then by contemplating God we shall learn nothing of practical use which we could not derive from contemplating nature. It sounds very grand and large-hearted to declaim of him

> *Who sees with equal eye, as God of all,*
> *A hero perish, or a sparrow fall,*
> *Atoms or systems into ruin hurl'd,*
> *And now a bubble burst, and now a world.*

How enjoyable it is to profess our enlightened acceptance of that cosmic will which

> *Lives through all life, extends through all extent,*
> *Spreads undivided, operates unspent,*
> *Breathes in our soul, informs our mortal part,*
> *As full, as perfect in a hair, as heart,*
> *As full, as perfect in vile Man that mourns*
> *As the rapt seraph that adores and burns.*
> *To him no high, no low, no great, no small:*
> *He fills, he bounds, connects, and equals all.*

These are fine sentiments incomparably expressed: but what is the practical conclusion?

> *Hearing this descant on omnipotence*
> *'So what?' interpolates our practic sense.*
> *Wisdom replies: Presume not God to scan,*
> *The proper study of mankind is man.*

Precisely. If God is everything, we can make our bow to him, and get on with the business of being something.

Is this the inevitable progress of theology? Must man begin with a fertile but superstitious idolatry of archetypes, reduce the archetypes to creative intentions in one supreme will, and then agree to know nothing about him, except that everything expresses him? We have certainly got to move forward from archetypes to universality, but is the negative road the only road that can be taken? There is another road, and Scripture describes it: it is the road by which God himself has been pleased to lead us. Let us consider it with the greatest possible brevity; and let us, for that purpose, go back again to the beginning of the road, the place where the archetypal images stand.

The archetypes, however heathenish they look, hold the promise of revelation. Of Jehovah the King, King David is the instrument; then David's righteous acts are as the acts of God: and if God manifestly acts, that is revelation. David's kingdom failed most evidently to express either the holiness or the power of the God whom Israel knew. This being so, several developments were possible. Crass heathenism would have reduced the image of God to the scale of David. Enlightened rationalism would have abandoned the kingly archetype, and cut the thread connecting God with the throne. The soul of Israel, in the end, did neither: it saw in David the foreshadowing of a holy and universal kingdom in which the Kingdom of God should be adequately expressed. Religion became faith, and looked forward.

But how could that which faith hoped for possibly be realized? The divine King revealed in the kingdom of David would not do, because the kingdom of David was simply a part of nature; it was a thread in the woof of history, and history is a cobweb in the enormous edifice of the world. But suppose that God should act in another way; suppose he should introduce a shining thread into the web, a new David, whose existence should be no mere part of nature, but the supernaturalization of a natural life, by the taking of it into God? God broke the old kingdom of David through the folly of the kings, the stubbornness of the tribes, and the sword of Nebuchadnezzar, and out of great tribulation he brought a new David, the Son of Man.

If we set out from the place of the old archetypes, there are only two roads we can follow. If human reason is our guide, we must take the negative road, reduce the archetypes to creative intentions, and merge them in the creating mind. This is as much a retreat as it is an advance: an advance in reason and liberty, a retreat from the hope of seeing God. An unequivocal advance does not lie in our power, but only in the power of the God our faith desires to see. An advance from the place of archetypes is only possible by the enhancement of the archetypal relation to a relation of identity. Thou shalt not make to thyself a graven image: God cannot be revealed in picture or in effigy, whether the effigy be a golden calf under Sinai or David enthroned at Jerusalem. No half-measures are possible: only if the image comes alive, if the pictured deity steps down from the golden frame, if God is incarnate, can we say with St. John: We know that the Son of God is come; this is the true God, and eternal life; my children, keep yourselves from idols.

When we, from our cool place of historical detachment, study the world of primitive religion, we may speak of the archetypal relation between the God and the king. But to the primitive believer the relation is always more than archetypal, there is a real identity there, at least an identity of action. The Lord's anointed is a present God, or the hand of God. The archetypal relation must be pressed in the direction of identity: it is not good enough to say that the Lord's heavenly throne is the archetype of the mercy-seat in the temple: we must say that in some manner he is enthroned on Zion, or the cultus becomes an absurdity. There are, in fact, only two ways in which the archetypal relation can be treated as a dynamic identity: either God must be naturalized, or his expressive instrument must be supernaturalized. God cannot be naturalized, man can merely feign it. But God's instrument can be supernaturalized, for God can effect it. To naturalize God is idolatry: for God to supernaturalize his instrument is incarnation. The religion of Israel was neither idolatry nor incarnation, but a suspense between the two. The religion of the Gentiles tends also to hang in suspense: not so often, however, between idolatry and incarnation, as between idolatry and theistic rationalism. And in so far as modern Judaism loses the Messianic Hope, it must conform, in this respect, to the Gentile type. Let us not, however, be too ready with that reproach,

since much that passes for Christianity is in the same predicament, poised between pure rational theology, and a superstitious reverence for a supposed human author to the Sermon
on the Mount.

Where there is paganism, genuine mythology can flourish.
God being finitized, finite images can properly express both
him and his doings. The acts of the archetypal and divine
king are the enlarged shadows of what his human image performs. Sometimes they coincide; when David assails the
Philistines, the God of battles descends and leads the van. At
this level, speech about God involves no philosophical problem. If the divine archetype is reduced to his human image,
why should he not be described in human terms? If we take
the negative road and move in the direction of pure theistic
rationalism, there is no great difficulty, either, in seeing what
will happen to the mythology: it will become platonized. The
archetypes have now been reduced to creative intentions in
the divine will. David reigned, and God willed David to
reign. Whatever is real or positive in David's kingly rule will,
no doubt, express a preceding divine intention: what the
intention was can be most usefully studied in the effect. We
shall, no doubt, view the providence which underlies history
as something more than the history; but for the theistic
rationalist to form a positive conception of this providence,
to give content to this divine thought, can never be a wholly
serious exercise. He will be more or less knowingly relapsing
into the old finite archetypal theology. He will do so, not
because he supposes that the result can have any proper truth,
but because (let us say) he wishes to adore the divine providence behind history. But you cannot adore a bare notion,
you cannot adore the fact that there is (presumably) providence. Providence must be bodied forth, it must be made
visible à la fantaisie if it is to be made *sensible au coeur*: so the
worshipper of historical providence will allow himself the
luxury of a model which is not an idol, an imaginative realiza-
tion without claims to particular truth.

The real philosophical problems about mythology arise when we take the other road, and advance under the leading of God from archetypes to incarnation. For here we shall be asserting in all seriousness that God, the true, the infinite God, is both intending and performing particular acts. How can his acts be seen, known, conceived or uttered? If the Lord acted through David his anointed, David's act was natural—the overthrow of Philistia—and God's act was the enlarged shadow of the natural and earthly act, projected upon the clouds. If God is, in Christ, reconciling the world to himself, there is not even a natural *starting-point*: for Christ's act in reconciling the world is not a natural action. He does the reconciling, indeed, by death, and the death of a man is certainly natural enough: we can all die presently, we need no more than leave off food and drink. But Christ's human death is not, of itself and in itself and as a natural event, the reconciliation of the world: what reconciles the world is an act of God fulfilled through the passion of man. This divine action is the supernatural thing. It is for us as vivid and particular and real a divine action as anything ever conveyed by mythology to a primitive mind. Did God descend from heaven to visit Baucis and Philemon? God visited no less particularly when he entered the virgin's womb. But while Jupiter had only to step down from a definable place above the glassy floor of heaven, the Eternal Word must be gathered from all immensity and begin in Mary to have a place. Even so to speak is to materialize eternal godhead: immensity is not gathered into Mary, but he who is neither immense nor measurable nor in any way conceivable by spatial extent takes place and body, when the Word of God is made flesh.

The ineffable thing happens: for why should not God do that of which man cannot speak? But man must also speak it; or how shall it be known and believed? Man cannot conceive it except in images: and these images must be divinely given to him, if he is to know a supernatural divine act. The images began to be given by Jesus Christ; the work was continued by the Spirit of Christ moving the minds of the Apostles. It was possible for Christ and the Apostles to use the images meaningfully, because the old archetypes were there to hand, already half transformed under the leading of God in the expectant faith of Israel. Christ clothed himself in the archetypal images, and then began to do and to suffer. The images were further transformed by what Christ suffered and did when he had put them on: they were transformed also by their all being combined in his one person. What sort of victorious David can it be, who is also the martyred Israel and the Lamb of sacrifice? What sort of new Adam can it be, who is also the temple of God? And what sort of living temple can it be, who is also the Word of God whereby the world was made?

The choice, use and combination of images made by Christ and the Spirit must be simply a supernatural work: otherwise Christianity is an illusion. Pagan superstition can believe crass mythology, and platonic myths can be handled with discretion by the poetical rationalist, but only God can make the figured representation by which is known for the first time 'what eye hath not seen nor ear heard, what hath not entered into the heart of man, whatsoever God hath prepared for them that love him'.

The Apostolic minds which developed and understood the images of faith performed a supernatural act: but supernatural acts, we remember, are continuous with natural functions, of which they are, so to speak, the upward prolongations. The boundary between the two need be neither objectively evident nor subjectively felt. The apostle would find himself to be performing a sort of activity well-known to the Rabbinic Jew, the activity of seeking fresh insights by the comparison and fusion of sacred images. Only now the images cluster round the central figures of Christ's self-revelation, and the insights sought from them are insights into Christ and his saving work. In his curiously mixed act of thought, half-poetic, half expository, the apostle might feel himself to be seized by the pentecostal Spirit and to undergo a control not his own. Yet such a seizure was neither the guarantee nor the condition of inspiration: not the guarantee, for compulsive thinking is of itself a purely psychological phenomenon: not the conditon, for God can supernaturally mould the thought of the saints apart from it. Inspiration is not a perceptible event.

The images are supernaturally formed, and supernaturally made intelligible to faith. Faith discerns not the images, but what the images signify: and yet we cannot discern it except *through* the images. We cannot by-pass the images to seize an imageless truth. Does this mean that our minds are simply given over to the images, bound hand and foot? Can we in any way criticize the images? Have we, outside them, any rule by which to regulate our intuition of what they mean?

Certainly we have a rule, a rule of a highly general kind, in the conception of God supplied to us by natural theology. The subject of the revealed figurative sentences is God: they must, then, be so understood that God can be the subject of them: and natural theology supplies us with a notion of God, itself analogical, it is true, but, as we said in a former lecture, composed of natural, and criticized, analogies, so that it can be settled and defined by a rational process. When we use this idea of the supreme being as a canon to interpret revelation, we are not importing into revelation something which was originally absent from it. On the contrary: guided and assisted by revealed insight, the apostles plainly did exercise that apprehension of the infinite creator through the works of nature which is the substance of natural knowledge. Had not Christ himself preached the God of nature to them from lilies and sparrows? The apostles were not, indeed, philosophers: but the philosophy of natural knowledge presupposes the knowledge it analyses and refines, and that natural knowledge, in abundant measure, the apostles had. What God bestowed on them through Christ was revelation of God's particular action. They had not known before that God would send his Son for us men and our salvation, but they had known that God was God; and what they now learnt was not that some superhuman Father had sent his Son, but that God had done so. Natural theology, then, provides a canon of interpretation which stands outside the particular matter of revealed truth.

Again, within the field of revealed truth, the principal images provide a canon to the lesser images. The reduction of the lesser images to terms of the greater is a theological activity, and we see it already proceeding in him who first earned the title of theologian, the 'divine' St. John. Christ, the Church taught, must come to be our judge. But, says St. John, his judging can be reduced to his coming: the light has only to come into the world, and it shows up the dark patches: and men's judgment is effected by their turning their back on the candle of the world. But when judgment is thus reduced to advent, it is not got rid of. If men are judged by seeing the face of God, they are judged, and their judgment is an additional truth to the truth of the vision, though now subordinated to it. St. John is not reducing everything to a confused simplicity. The images which he 'reduces' to terms of others no more disappear or lose their force, than do the whole body of images, when we remember that they are no more than images, and so reduce them to the one ineffable simplicity of God's saving love. All is denied, and all is affirmed: what the Christmas hymns say of God's descent to earth is the stammering of children's tongues, and nothing of it in accordance with the truth of that unspeakable mystery; and yet it is what God has taught us to say, when out of the mouths of babes he would establish praise. We speak because silence is impossible, and when we speak this is how we speak:

> *Behold the great Creator makes*
> *Himself a house of clay:*
> *A robe of virgin flesh he takes*
> *Which he will wear for ay.*

Hark, hark, the wise eternal Word
Like a weak infant cries:
In form of servant is the Lord
And God in cradle lies.

But now the high celestial throne
Ascribe we as is meet
To him, the Father's only Son,
Who breathes the Paraclete.

VII

O Lord, thou art stronger than I, and hast prevailed. If I say, I will not make mention of him, nor speak any more in his name, there is in my heart as it were a burning fire shut up in my bones, and I am weary with forbearing, I cannot contain. JEREMIAH, XX. 7-9

We have been trying to think about divine revelation, as we may see it happening in St. Paul or St. John, and we are driven back again and again to the same conclusion. The moving of these men's minds, or of any men's minds, by divine direction is in any case a profound and invisible mystery, as is the whole relation of the creature to the creator; but if we turn from the unfathomable depth to observe the surface, the perceptible process in the inspired mind, the psychological fact, then we may say that it is a process of images which live as it were by their own life and impose themselves with authority. They demand to be thought in this way or that, and not otherwise. Now such an account inevitably suggests a comparison with the inspiration of the poet; and to this comparison we will now turn, though with fear and trembling; for we all know what are the dangers lurking here. If we fall into doctrinal heresy we shall receive indulgent correction from the theologians, but if we attempt to define the poetic fact we shall wither under the scorn of those who show, both by teaching and example, that the Muse is in the melting-pot.

The Muse is in the melting-pot, and in what shape will she emerge from it? In her own shape rejuvenated? But has she a shape of her own, or is she a female Proteus, and unconfined to any special form? If so, is it any use talking of what she is, let alone comparing her with apostolic inspiration? If, when we begin to get our fingers round her feline elusiveness, she slips through them in a fish, a flame or a fountain, can we ever hope to hold her? Shall we ever compel her back into her proper visage, shall we ever wring oracular truth from this Old Woman of the Sea?

Is there, indeed, such a thing as poetry, or is every school and age of poetry, perhaps every poet, a distinct nature? The question is a perfectly possible question to ask. Theology, by hypothesis, is unchangeable in essence, for in spite of its various historical manifestations, it has to do with an eternal fact, the relation of the creature to the creator. But is there any deep and invariable necessity why men should spin verses, or why, if they do spin them, they should use them always for the same expressive purpose? Is poetry, like football, just what it happens at any time to be? For if football was first played in the streets of a town by unlimited numbers of boys, with rules based on the particular lay-out and hazards of the pavements and buildings, then football was not what it is now. All football, no doubt, is based on certain invariable facts, such as the aptitude of inflated bladders to bounce and to roll, and the tendency of immature males towards mimic conflict; but these invariable factors do not of themselves determine the nature of football. And poetry appears to be a free play of the mind, and a delight: and if some people have taken it in deadly earnest, what of it? Some people have taken football in earnest, and some people never grow up.

Poetry, like football, rests on certain invariable facts. Man expresses himself by language, and language, being repetitive noise, is capable of musical arrangement. Again, a man cannot apprehend anything without an act of imaginative creation. From these two invariable facts arise the two possibilities of playing freely with the musicality of words, and playing freely with imaginative creation; and out of these

two possibilities flows the third joint possibility of making
the musical game the expression of the imaginative game.
Such a joint form of game may not seem any more inevitable than other mixed forms, say opera or polo. And even
granting that men will mount upon the crests of verbal
rhythms to play at imaginative creation, it is, again, in no
way inevitable that anything serious should come of it; or
that if it does, it should fulfil one spiritual function rather
than another.

If we compare apostolic inspiration with poetry, it is no
doubt with great or serious poetry that we shall compare it.
According to some of our most admired contemporaries,
'Sing a Song of Sixpence' is poetry of the purest water; but it
offers no useful analogy to the Gospel of St. Mark or the
Revelation of St. John. If only we were concerned with 'Sing
a Song of Sixpence' we might claim to be dealing with the
eternal essence of poetry, for this sort of thing has been going
on since men and blackbirds first began to sing. It is precisely
the serious poetry that is so time-conditioned. If I ask myself
about the nature of serious poetry, I shall very likely find
myself reflecting on what the English poets were doing from
Spenser until some time after Keats, from the Renaissance,
that is, until the Renaissance Muse began to feel desperately
used up, and ready for a plunge into Medea's pot; where they
are, let us hope, cooking her up into a fresh youth. But is the
spiritual function of great poetry from Spenser to Keats the
spiritual function of great poetry, or just the spiritual function
of great poetry from Spenser to Keats?

We can, of course, compare what St. John was doing with
what Shakespeare was doing, but that will not be to compare
the essence of inspiration with the essence of great poetry, it
will be to compare St. John and Shakespeare, a comparison
which may have a limited interest. If I do talk about comparing the essence of apostolic inspiration with the essence of
great poetry, I am suggesting that one might compare the
inspired writing St. John produced with the great poetry he

might have produced if he had been the recipient of a different sort of gift. Here indeed is a fascinating speculation: let us indulge it a little.

St. John is to be a poet; shall he write in Hebrew, or in Greek? Since we are ignorant of Hebrew, let us plunge for Scylla and shun Charybdis by all means; he shall write in Greek. What medium did the Greek of his time offer to such a poet? The Classical Greek convention was then far more certainly used up and spent than the Renaissance convention is now. If it is now difficult to write heroic lines without appearing to parody Dryden or Pope, it was far more difficult then to write hexameters without parodying Homer or Hesiod. The convention of language limited the subject-matter: if one wrote the old measures, one refined on the old themes. To such a man as St. John, standing outside the academic Classical culture, and in the shadow of the synagogue, the composition of Homeric hexameters could scarcely be the vehicle for great poetry; if you want to see the sort of thing likely to result from the attempt, you may read, if you do not fall asleep in the middle, a page of the Jewish pseudo-Sibylline Oracles. What, then, could he do? He must presumably begin a new poetry out of the rhythms of prose. And here he would be more fortunate, for the popular rhetoric of his period had developed an ornate and musical style, with clauses carefully balanced in cadence and length. And these rhythms would easily combine in his head with the balanced clauses of the old Hebrew poetry, as that poetry could be felt even through the jagged barbarity of the current Greek version. What sort of thing, then, should we expect him to write?

> *These are they . that issue*
> *from the great . tribulation:*
> *Who have washed . their garments*
> *and who have . whitened them*
> *in the blood . of the Lamb.*

Therefore are they . in presence
of the throne . of God:
And do him . service
both by day . and by night
within his . sanctuary.

In any case St. John's poetry would have to be a rhythmical prose; the lines need scarcely have differed from the loftiest phrases of his actual prose writings. So much for manner; now for the matter. For however an inspired apostle and a poet may coincide in style, their functions are surely very different. Well: but so far as matter is concerned, St. John is decisively attached to the Jewish tradition, and not the Greek. If, then, an Israelite wrote great or serious poetry, what was it like? An Israelite might certainly write simple love-ditties, or simple dirges, or drinking songs. But great poetry, I take it, is supposed to express something more complex than a simple emotion of love, grief or pleasure: it is supposed to express the texture of human existence, or the predicament of man. Could the Israelite do this except by way of psalm, or prophecy, or prayer, or devout meditation, or theological epic? Is great poetry, in the sense in which Shakespearian tragedy is great, conceivable in Israel, otherwise than as sacred utterance? And is Israel singular in this regard? Can one suppose that any really primitive people could have a great and deep poetry which was not religious? If not, we may wonder whether we have been asking the right question. Should we ask what is the relation between religious inspiration and great poetry, or should we not rather ask how the inspiration of great poetry ever came to be secularized?

As a mere fact of historical process, we can see the secularization take place under our very eyes. In the pagan classical culture, mythological epic and ritual drama were progressively humanized. Gradually the poets cease to write about the gods as real persons who govern or intervene, and must be served and propitiated: they become names for the aspects of human destiny. Aphrodite is no longer anything but the passion of love itself. But in so far as this passion is still personified and divinized, a common essence is felt to be expressed in all loving. This gives the poets something to write about. They are not novelists, elaborating the simply particular: they are poets, expressing a common essence extending through multiple experience. The Christian and Renaissance poets clung to the figures of the classical gods, which, though theologically unreal, were real poetically, since they expressed the essences which were still the subject of poetry. Keats wrote an ode to the god Autumnus, not a description of an autumn day; the personification holds together the various autumnal features in a single essence which, without the personification, would fall to pieces. Shelley invents an endless new mythology, the spirit of this, and the spirit of that: soberer minds have been content with a single goddess, Nature.

Now in our day, perhaps, the Olympian gods who suffered a theological death sixteen hundred years ago, are undergoing poetical death, their last dissolution. This may be a fact of higher importance than appears. Whether the poets have now got any essences to write about, and whether, in the lack of them, they will be driven either into prose, nursery rhymes, or true religion, I would not venture to suggest. The Muse is in the melting-pot, and I cannot see what is happening to her: though I do seem to catch glimpses of some severely theological shapes forming here and there in the molten mass.

Those of us who are not quite up to the guessing-game around the melting-pot, form our instinctive opinion of poetry from the happy post-Renaissance period, so let us return to that. It seems that the great poets of this period wrote with an implicit faith, of which they might be wholly unaware, in human existence as something infinitely deep and rich, and as having a common essence throughout. One took up some symbol which for any reason obtruded itself, whether the figure of a dead god or the story of a Danish prince, or

some more common object of natural experience, and one
set it moving by poetical incantation. It moved, it controlled
the words, it insisted on acting and expressing itself in one
way and not another. The resultant verse had a certain inevitability: that was the thing. One reads it and says that it is
right, or true. Right or true about what? Not simply about
the particular object, whatever it may be, of the poet's imaginative experience—when we say that it is true we are not
simply saying that something has really been imagined, and
that the imagination has really been expressed. We are saying
that, no doubt, but we are saying also that the expressed
imagination has great and wide symbolizing power. It is a
sort of focus into which is drawn together much that seems to
us most important in the common essence of our human existence. The phrase which is just right has infinite overtones: or
it awakens echoes in all the hidden caves of our minds.

The problem of the meaning of such poetry cannot be
understood in independence of the problem of meaning in
general. How any word succeeds in meaning anything is a
mystery which almost defeats philosophy on the threshold of
her enquiry. A word is, of itself, simply a sound in my mouth
or the shadow of a sound in my brain. Yet I use it with
significance—because, we may think, the imaginative representation of that to which the word refers accompanies the
word. But this simply is not true. Even if I say something
simple, like 'dog', I am not commonly aware of any imaginary dog trotting in the field of fantasy; and if I use the
name of something highly complicated, like 'post-renaissance
poetry', there is no question of a corresponding object being
represented in imagination. What I feel inclined to say is that
when I use the expression I pick up, as it were, a complicated
knot, in which are ready tied together threads running to all
that variety of ideas for which 'post-renaissance poetry' is the
shorthand expression. Thus, if I say the expression and know
what I am saying, I have got all the threads in my hand; and
I can easily follow any of them I like back to the idea to which

it leads. And this is true; having used the expression, I can follow it up by looking at one after another of the particulars to which it refers. But my power to take up, in further acts of thought, the references of a word, does not explain in any way how the word is significant now: the fact that I could perform further acts of thought (but may not actually trouble to do so) cannot explain the nature of the act of thought I am performing now. It seems necessary to swallow the mystery, and to say that the things the word means are sufficiently present to our minds to put meaning into the word, but not sufficiently present to clutter up our mental vision with a mass of distinct detail. They are fully present, in fact, through and in our act of using the word, not alongside of it.

In the case of our ordinary practical or logical thinking, it may indeed be hard to say just what threads of meaning any word touches, but anyhow our object is to limit and define meaning: words with vague and indeterminate suggestions are liable to be a nuisance. But it would seem that the words of a poem have an opposite purpose, and are intended to arouse all possible echoes. Of course the poetical line must have a *prima facie* meaning which is fairly simple and determinate like any other sentence: according to the *prima facie* sense we are listening to Hamlet talking about waking and sleeping. But according to a secondary or symbolical significance, the line suggests the repulsion and attraction of death to Hamlet, and Hamlet, placed as he is and feeling as he does, becomes the symbol of heaven knows how much.

Those who revolt from any suggestion that poetry has a symbolical sense are revolting, principally, perhaps, from the suggestion that the symbolical sense can be *stated*, in a number of sentences other than those of the poem itself; and with this objection we may agree. What the poem presents to us is simply two things—first, the literal and obvious sense, whatever that may be, and second, whatever echoes of human nature or destiny or the like the poetry does in fact evoke. But it is with the poetical words as it is with any other words—what they primarily signify is expressed in them, not along-side of them. It is in the act of discourse or of understanding discourse that we apprehend. Though what we apprehend is not the words, what we apprehend is stated in the words; there is no getting behind that mysterious fact. So if I read the words of Hamlet it is in reading those words that I apprehend, first, the imaginary person and predicament of Hamlet, second, whatever of human existence is focussed in Hamlet. It is with the second and vaguer apprehension that we are concerned when we are talking of the high inspiration of great poetry. The mind apprehends life in talking about it, and for the most part we talk about it piecemeal and with some exactitude, and that is the most useful way of appre-hending our life for practical purposes. But in talking the language of Hamlet we may grasp our existence or the possi-bilities of our existence over a wide area and in a richer and more confused way. If we ask just *what* we are grasping, we are returning to the prosaic form of thought and the poetry vanishes.

I know the appalling rashness of such generalizations as that which I have just thrown out; and no doubt it is true, if at all, about some of the significance of some great poetry, and has no right to pass as a general description. Still, if we are trying to compare the inspiration of our apostle with the poetry of a post-renaissance poet, we must generalize in some way about the poetry, and here is the generalization we have thought fit to make.

Let us now advance a step further, and ask what must have been happening in the poet's mind if he is to produce poetry having the sort of power which we have attempted to describe. Consciously, perhaps, he is only setting images in motion by rhythmical incantation, and then appreciating a certain way in which they 'ought' to develop and to express themselves. It is this 'ought' which is the heart of the riddle. The poet does not know what sort of an 'ought' it is, except that it is the 'ought' with which his craft is concerned, and that he is able to feel and acknowledge it. But what the poet assumes, the philosopher investigates. We need not here, perhaps, take the investigation very far. It may be enough to say that since, by our hypothesis, the poet is going to produce a symbol powerfully expressive of a deep quality in human existence, what he must feel in the 'ought' is the quality of human existence clamouring for expression and, as it were, pressing upon his mind and directing the manipulation of the poetical symbols. The poet's imagination is responsive to the possibilities of destiny in general as well as to the particular possibility of destiny realized in Hamlet: that is why he sees that he ought to make Hamlet speak as he does, and not otherwise.

Let us say, then, that the post-renaissance poet is responsive to qualities or patterns of human existence. But here the theologian or even the metaphysician within us is likely to awake, and to say that the actual quality or pattern of our existence is determined by our place in a system of being which transcends ourselves: that in all our existence we are conforming to or falsifying the relation of a creature to its creator, we are denying or actualizing a nature which has been assigned to us, we are either pretending to be angels or trying to be beasts, in one direction or another we are forcing the clauses of the charter of our creation. If the poets are sensitive to the qualities of existence, are they or are they not sensitive to all this? Everyone knows the answer: for the most part they are not, or anyhow not directly. There is a subjective bias about post-renaissance poetry; that to which the poets are responsive, that of which their great poetry is the effective symbol, is life as it is lived and felt by a sensitive and capacious mind. Theological symbols may be found in it, but all they show us at the most is how men think or feel about their destiny in the crises of it: what they say about their relation to God, and not what that relation really is, nor even how what they say compares with the theological truth.

This subjective or human bias is so strong that even poets who have the will to be theological and objective cannot bring it off. Milton ought, according to his own lights, to be showing us two things about Satan: first, how Satan, the proud and rebellious will, thinks of his relation to God, second, how what Satan thinks compares with the truth of his relation to God. And Milton tries to do both things: but according to the experience of most readers, he does not succeed in making such poetry of the second thing, as he does of the first. Satan, the rebel, is a tragic hero, expressing what sort of reaction an indomitable will both beaten and in the wrong can make; which is, further, a particular expression and symbol of the quality of the human will at all times. So much is great poetry: but the true relation of a created will to the creator, and the way in which Satan falsifies that relation, these matters are eloquently stated by Milton, but they do not live with the same poetical life. The mind which reads the poem does not tingle with a sense of the invisible cord binding creature to creator, a cord which we can throttle ourselves by struggling with, but can never break. What the reader's veins do tingle with is the titanic quality of Satan's will.

People say habitually that poetry is not moral, still less theological, truth, it is just life; and we can see well enough what the remark means when it is applied to post-renaissance poetry. But then we could almost have known *a priori* that it would be so, for the post-renaissance culture was as a whole devoted to the intoxicating task of exploring the length and the breadth, the depth and the height, of the microcosm man. If the poetry of such an age is 'just life' in the sense intended, it hardly follows that the poetry of every other age will have to be 'just life', too. It may well follow, indeed, that those who have made the post-renaissance attitude their own will not be able to feel the poetical force of any other poetry, or will only be able to feel it in so far as they can humanize it: but that does not prove that only humanistic poetry is possible,

nor that all non-humanistic poetry is really aiming at human-
ism, even though it has not arrived there.

The speeches of the Almighty in *Paradise Lost* are not great
poetry, and one feels about them as one feels about the little
heavens appearing in the right-hand top corners of baroque
pictures—they are not the principal thing. But the speeches of
the Almighty in the Hebrew prophets are the principal thing,
in fact they are the whole thing: some of them have a claim
to be great poetry, and it is very difficult to humanize them
or to say that they are 'just life'. The unreclaimed humanist in
all of us may bathe in the court-history of King David, and
when we come to 'Would God that I had died for thee, O
Absalom, my son, my son', we feel that we are getting our
familiar food. But we must also have a faint awareness that
we are being allowed a holiday from the proper business of
the Old Testament Muse.

But what is the humanist going to do with this?

'Wherefore I will yet plead with you, saith the Lord; and
with your children's children will I plead. For pass over to the
coasts of Kittim, and see; and send unto Kedar, and consider
diligently; and see if there hath been such a thing. Hath a
nation changed gods, which are yet no gods? But my people
hath changed their glory for that which profiteth not. Be
astonished, O heavens, at this, and be horribly afraid; be
utterly desolate, saith the Lord. For my people hath committed two evils: they have forsaken me, the fountain of living
waters; and hewed them out cisterns, broken cisterns that can
hold no water.'

According to the humanist formula these lines must presumably express what it feels like to be the member of a people
which, falling into bad luck, experiences a superstitious
remorse about its neglect of the tribal God. But to say this is
to twist Jeremiah's lines. Shakespeare knew that he was writing about human life: Milton tried to go higher, but could
not always; then he failed by an inward and strictly poetic
test. But Jeremiah is not, in his own intention, writing about

human life, but about the Lord God of Israel; and he does not fail by the inward test, we do not see him slipping off the point; we see no evidence of a painful and unconvincing effort to keep the image of God in the centre of the picture. On the contrary, there is a painful effort from time to time to obtrude Jeremiah's private hopes, fears, and recalcitrances; but they are forced back, trampled, annihilated by the Word of God.

If we permit ourselves to think of Jeremiah as a poet, as a man who sets images moving by musical incantation, and allows them to arrange and express themselves as they *ought*, then what are we to say about his *ought*? Partly, like any poet's *ought*, it will be a matter of right musical arrangement, of consistency and force in the images themselves: but that will not be all. The post-renaissance poet, we suppose, experienced in the *ought* of his craft the pressure of life—what it is to be a man, and alive, and up against destiny, and so on. If it is not 'just life' which presses Jeremiah, then what is it that presses him, and constrains his images?

It is impossible, I am afraid, to answer this question without betraying some definite metaphysical assumptions. If we accept Jeremiah's own assumptions, all is plain. What constrains his images is the particular self-fulfilling will of God, perceptible in the external events of history and nature which God controls, perceptible also in a direct impact upon Jeremiah's inspired mind. If we are not prepared to believe in the perceptibly expressed particular divine will, we can still make some sense of Jeremiah's poetry, so long as we grant an eternal creative act from which the creature cannot escape. If we grant that the self-will of the creature can be experienced by the creature as a straining of its bond with the creative act, then we can say that the prophet dramatizes the ineluctable hold of the creator, and the self-punishment of our rebellions; he casts into personal and mythological form the ever varying revenges of eternal Truth upon our restless infidelities. But if we will not concede even this: if there is no ineluctable

125

nature of things except, let us say, economic and political realities, against which Israel rebels: if the only forces of destiny are soulless and lower than man himself, if that from which Israel turns away is not, in any case, a fountain of living waters: then we must say that Jeremiah's poetry corresponds to a visionary and fanatical idolatry only: and if the negations which our lips profess are operative in us at an imaginative level, we shall not even begin to experience Jeremiah's lines as great poetry.

So far we have been stretching the name of poetry as widely as we can: we have attempted to think of Hebrew prophecy and post-renaissance poetry as coming under the same general description as two varieties of poetry: only, we have said, what presses on the poet, what makes his 'ought', differs in the two cases. But the difference between the two controlling pressures is enormous, and it has such important consequences, that when we have taken them into account we may no longer wish to retain prophecy as a species of poetry.

Let us note first that the control of reality over the post-renaissance poet, just because it works subjectively, is infinitely elastic. If we are responding to the quality of human existence, subjectively considered, we can imagine and devise the freest of fictions: we can place Miranda in her magic island, and see what she must do and say in such conditions. There has to be a 'must' or there can be no great poetry, but the 'must' merely tells us what the imaginative experiment in human existence *must* be, to be human. It stops us making our invention inconsistent or frigid, it does not stop us inventing. And this fact has given poetry its name: the poet is a 'maker'. Whereas Jeremiah is not in any sense a 'maker'. He is not stretching this way and that the elastic possibilities of human nature. His objective control does not limit the evolutions of any puppets freely made by fancy: his control tells him exactly what to say, for he is not responding to the quality of human life, he is responding to the demands of eternal will on Israel as they make themselves heard in the determinate situation where he stands.

We do meet the self-conscious poet, the 'maker', in the Old Testament—and we find him somewhat incongruous. 'My tongue is the pen of a ready writer,' he declares: 'I recite the things I have *made* upon the King.' He is, in fact, a laureate who has made up a piece of jewelled rhetoric for the marriage of some Ahab to some Jezebel. He is a *maker*, as truly as was any loyal Elizabethan sonneteer; but there is nothing great about the performance. For greatness we may turn to Jeremiah: and there is the greatness, but it is not a 'making'. The Old Testament will supply us with mixed cases, halfway between the 'making' of the psalm *Eructavit* and the prophecy of Jeremiah, for example, the book of Job: but it is the pure case we can most profitably study.

To take now a second difference. We said some while back that we cannot distinguish in post-renaissance poetry between the symbol, that is, the expressed poem, and its 'message', as old-fashioned people used to say. Qualities and possibilities of human existence, vaguely felt or anticipated in many parts of our minds, find expression in the poem. The poem expresses whatever of the infinite aspects of human existence it does express: what it does not express, it leaves unexpressed. One can never say 'The poet ought to have been saying so and so, but he has only succeeded in saying this'. There is nothing that he ought to have been saying except what he has said. All life is open to him: let him say what the Muse prompts him to say. He may not say much, or he may not say it well, but he cannot say the wrong thing. And what he says is said in the poem: it cannot be put into other words, for other words would evoke different echoes, and would be an expression of different qualities of existence (if of any).

The case of the prophet is not, anyhow, this. What he has got to say is determinate and particular, it is what the Lord God declares and requires on the day on which he speaks. It is designed to evoke not an exquisite and contemplative realiza-

tion of human existence, but particular practical responses to
God. For this reason it can be put into other words: whether
we say 'They have deserted me, the fountain of living waters,
and hewed them out cisterns,' or say 'They have turned their
back on the living God, and made to themselves graven
images' the same essential truth is expressed; even though the
poetical evocations of 'the fountain of living waters' are infinite, and that expression is far more moving than the other.
Indeed, the prophet's message might be translated into the
flattest of prose, without completely evaporating: though
almost nothing that the prophets say in God's name is flat
prose. Still, if the prophecy can be put into prose and the
poem cannot, does not this seem to show that the poetical
character of the prophetic utterance is immaterial—that the
prophet is really just a rhetorician, who knows what the substance of his message must be first, and then colours it up with
the flowers of speech to make it effective? No, if anything can
be known about the prophets at all, this, anyhow, can be
known to be false. It is the other way about: poetry, for the
prophet, is a technique of divination, in the poetic process he
gets his message.

The prophets used, at various times, several divinatory
techniques; the more primitive and dramatic of them were
handled with great understanding and knowledge by a recent
Bampton Lecturer. The prophet divined from what he saw
when he looked out of a window, he divined from chance
words overheard. An investigation into such divinatory prac-
tices is of the highest interest, but it leaves us always with one
unsatisfactory reflection. Even the great prophets used these
devices from time to time: Jeremiah himself divined from the
chance sight of a budding almond, and of a boiling pot. But
for the most part the great prophets used no such methods:
they simply had their minds charged with the word of God.
But in such a case, what happened? Is not the answer really
obvious, that poetry itself was the method of divination?
Whatever signs or omens set the incantation of shapely words

moving in the prophet's mind, it went on moving and forming itself with a felt inevitability, like that of a rhapsodical
poetry which allows for no second thoughts: it formed itself
under a pressure or control which the prophet experienced as
no self-chosen direction of his own thinking, but as the constraint of a divine will. As the prophet speaks his own person
is lost, and the person whose utterance the words express becomes the person of the Lord. If this had not been the
prophet's experience he would never have dared to give his
words as the words of a God who avenged falsification with
death, nor would he have been so utterly shattered when
what gave itself to him as the Lord's word appeared to be
refuted by the event.

What the prophet shares with the latter-day poet, then, is
the technique of inspiration chiefly: both move an incantation
of images under a control. The controls are not the same, and
therefore the whole nature and purpose of the two utterances
go widely apart: the poet is a maker, the prophet is a mouth-
piece.

Everything that we have said, either about the poet or the
prophet, will be likely to cause the psychologist nothing but
quiet amusement. He will say something of this sort. When
we control our speech by logic and common-sense and constant reference to practical experience, we can keep it objective, but when we set going an imaginative incantation and
let what will control it, then the psychologist knows what
will happen. The control will be exercised by the non-
rational forces of the unconscious or subconscious mind. This
objection opens the door on an endless discussion in which I
am neither willing nor competent to engage. I must content
myself with forcing the door to again with a single philosophical generality. Our psychological make-up is admittedly
an instrument of the most baffling complexity, liable to all
sorts of disorders, and certain to colour whatever passes
through it. There will be something for the psychologist to
study in Shakespeare and in Jeremiah: and indeed the province

has not been neglected. But are we to conclude that the way-wardness of our psyche prevents reality from exerting any real pressure or constraint upon us, except in so far as we bully and regiment her by hard logic and hard practicality? Does the reality of our friends not shine through our free emotional reactions to them? Do we see men most really when we let ourselves love them, and even poetize a bit about them, when we let our minds free to respond to them, or when we take them to pieces with analytical exactitude? If there is objective reality in the poetizing of love, in spite of all its riot of subjec-tivity, then there seems no reason why the apparent greatness of Shakespeare's poetry should not have something to do with realities of human existence pressing and constraining his fictions: nor is the question of the reality of the divine constraint on Jeremiah's mind excluded by anything we know.

We have been driven into an examination of Hebrew pro-phecy, because we wanted to know what sort of poetry St. John would write if he wrote it. We thought it would be more in the nature of great Hebrew poetry than of post-renaissance poetry: so we examined the great Hebrew poet, and found him to be a prophet, and therefore, not properly a poet at all. Shall we say, then, that St. John is a prophet? If we do, we shall receive confirmation from St. John's familiar angel. I am a fellow-servant, says this angel, with thee, and with thy brethren that have the testimony of Jesus: for the testimony of Jesus is the spirit of your prophecy.

No one, surely, can talk about such mysteries of the mind as we have discussed without knowing that he is talking non-sense. There is no question here of proper and exact state-ment, of a theory of poetry or of prophetical inspiration. All we can do is to distinguish certain real differences, and evoke the inscrutableness, even in our own minds, of the making word. What then shall we say of that word whereby the world was made, or of that utterance more high and more divine, of which the effect as well as the begetter is Almighty

God, whereby that Son is constituted in being, of whom it is written, 'His generation who shall declare?' *To whom, therefore, with the Father and the Holy Ghost, be ascribed, as is most justly due, all might, dominion, majesty and power henceforth and for ever.*

VIII

The voice said, Go, take the book which is open in the hand of the angel that standeth upon the sea and the land. And I went unto the angel, bidding him to give me the book. And he said to me, Take it, and devour it. APOCALYPSE, X. 8-9

In this last lecture we must try to draw several threads together and say what we have to say about the movement of inspiration in apostolic minds. We have compared the inspiration of the New Testament with the inspiration of the ancient prophets and with the inspiration (so called) of great poets. We have said something about the prophets and the poets, but about the apostolic writers almost nothing at all. It is in the apostolic field that we need now to apply and work out the comparison.

Let us start by tidying up an apparent inconsistency. A good way back we said about St. Paul and St. John that they reveal divine truth to us under the form of certain master-images: we gave the example of the Trinity. It was this observation which sent us off on a wide detour, examining the function of images in metaphysics, rational theology, poetry and prophecy. And while all the suggested comparisons proved relevant, the comparison with prophecy was obviously the closest: indeed, we quoted St. John's own testimony to show that he regarded his own inspiration as prophetical. What, then, is the inconsistency? It is this: we thought of the divine control over St. Paul or St. John as developing the images in his mind: the images were the matter of revelation. Whereas in talking of Jeremiah we suggested that the poetical and imaged form was rather a technique of divination than the

matter of revelation: in fact, we said, one could translate
from image to image, or even into cold prose, without
destroying the content. Here, then, we seem to have got
prophets whose images are inessential to their message, and
prophetical apostles whose images are the substance of what
they reveal. But, if this is really so, then the comparison between prophet and apostle cannot be so close as we supposed,
and the distance which opens between them touches the very
point which is most vital to us, the quasi-poetical movement
of images in the inspired mind.

For light upon this difficulty let us return to Jeremiah. We
used as our example one of those oracles in which the divine
voice pleads with Israel. 'They have deserted me, the fountain
of living waters.' The substance of the reproach, we said,
could be alternatively expressed, and, we might add, does
receive in the prophets a great number of equivalent expressions. Yes, but behind all such alterable images there remain
the images which cannot be altered. Behind all divine pleas
and reproaches there stand the images which give them their
sense and bearing: the image of the God who is as man and
not as man: the image of the divine word, a spell which
makes and mars all human things: the image of the covenant
made on such strange terms between God and Israel under
Mount Sinai: the image of divine indwelling in the hill of
Zion, which is yet only a shadow of a heavenly enthronement:
these and so many other images besides. Apart from them the
divine pleading and threatening which flowed in sublime
poetry through the prophet's brain would have no meaning
at all. In the prophets, as in the apostles, we must distinguish
between the master-images for which there are no equiva-
lents, and the subordinate images by which the master-images
are set forth or brought to bear.

Is this a sufficient clarification of our difficulty? Not quite.
We must certainly allow for the unalterable figures, the axio-
matic images of faith, which stand behind all the prophet's
particular oracles. But they stand behind, that is precisely the

difference. Whereas in the apostles the great images of faith are being freshly minted and reborn through Christ's incarnation, in the prophets they undergo no such transformation. It is not the images, nor anything about the substance of the images, that is being revealed in the prophets: the images are taken for granted, and something else is revealed on the basis of them: the particular warnings and pleadings of God.

It is impossible for any Christian, I should even say, for any historian, to deny altogether the validity of such a distinction. The prophets were not publishing a new religion, the apostles were. The appearance of a new religion, and the transformation of basic images, are not simply connected things: they are one and the same thing. There was a crisis of images in the experience of the witnesses to the incarnation which cannot in any case be paralleled in the experience of the prophets. The results are visible in the two sets of writings: the apostles know that they are transforming the images by referring them to Christ, or rather, that Christ has transformed them, by clothing himself with them and dying in the armour. The prophets are not aware of any such transformation: so far as the fundamental images of their faith are concerned, they see themselves for the most part as pure traditionalists, appealing over the head of a degenerate and paganized monarchy back to Moses and David.

Nevertheless we cannot say that the revelation through prophets was not a revelation of fundamental images, but merely of something else erected on the basis of them. It is absurd to say that the great images are 'taken for granted', or that they are buried presuppositions. It is the images themselves that thunder and lighten in the prophetic oracles. It is the covenant, the word, the divine kingship, the session on the mercy-seat, that burst forth with threatening, persuasion and hope, by way of reaction to the abominations of Israelite apostasy and the movements of Chaldaean conquest. The images of faith do not only reveal themselves freshly when they are undergoing alteration: they reveal themselves continually by always being alive. We may compare our own experience: divine mercy is always the same, we are receiving no new revelation about it. Yet in being always the same it is always new; try as we may we cannot take it for granted. Every reconciliation to which Mercy brings our foolish will is a new miracle: it is as familiar and as unexpected as the greenness of each succeeding spring.

Thus the divine pleadings in the prophets reveal the images of faith for what they are, and have always been. Yet this is not the whole truth. For the fundamental images do not simply remain what they have always been in the prophets: in being expressed and applied, they change their nature very gradually, and as it were invisibly. For the religion of Israel, considered as a total phenomenon, was always in suspense between idolatry and incarnation: and the breath of inspiration in it blew always towards incarnation and away from idolatry. For this reason the fundamental images are being continually and imperceptibly reinterpreted in the direction of a supernatural sense, even though the prophets themselves do not know it. The presence and act of deity so fill the images that all past or contemporary embodiments of them are rejected: God must make a *new* covenant, he must circumcise the *heart*, he must raise up a *new* David, the earthly vessel of heavenly grace must be made worthy of it; not by itself, but by grace. The prophets do not know that the images are changing their natures—they do not know that the true temple will have to be no temple, but the flesh of the Virgin's Child. But they are so purifying and exalting the image that nothing merely natural will ever be able to embody it. In this sense the great images themselves are undergoing change in the prophets: and the act of soul by which this happens in them is a supernatural act, it is the process of the incarnation of God preparing its own way and casting its shadow before.

It is not, then, that a slight change of basic images was revealed in the prophets, and a different and greater change in the apostles. There is only one change: in the prophets the images are prepared for this change by being detached from their earthly moorings and drawn back into the hands of God; in the apostles we see the images already refashioned by the fingers of the divine potter. In the prophets the image of the kingdom is driven towards the clouds: in the gospel the clouds are parted, and the kingdom comes down in the Son of Man.

We see, then, that there are both in the prophets and apostles master-images and subordinate images. The master-images are undergoing change in both prophets and apostles, but not in the same manner or degree. Neither prophets nor apostles are inspired to devise simply new master-images. That is an impossibility. It is only through images already implanted that revelation grows. But the images, in growing, are transformed, they throw out fresh branches, they fertilize neighbouring and as yet purely natural imaginations.

Let us now leave the special problem we propounded concerning the prophets and the apostles. Whatever differences have to be acknowledged, they do not bear on the point we are just now most concerned to make: prophets and apostles alike are inspired by a quasi-poetical movement of images. I wish now to illustrate the quasi-poetical character to be found in the New Testament writings: I wish to show that the sort of criticism of most use for getting to the bottom of the New Testament is often more like the criticism we apply to poetry than we might incline to expect.

I will take one of the most famous and the most discussed of critical problems, the ending of St. Mark. We all know that the last twelve verses of this gospel, as they are printed in our bibles, have no defensible claim to be genuine. They were added by a competent scribe to round the story off and bring it into parallel with the conclusions of the other gospels. We know that the other evangelists read St. Mark before they wrote their own books, and the evidence strongly suggests that they had no more of St. Mark before them than we have: their Mark ended where our genuine Mark ends, with the flight of the women from the empty sepulchre. So we ask ourselves whether St. Mark in fact ever wrote, or meant to write, any more. There is, of course, no difficulty in supposing that just as St. Mark reached the words 'for they were afraid', a heavy hand descended on his shoulder, and a heavy official voice pronounced the fateful words: 'Here, what's all this? You'd better come along with me to the pretorium,' and so the saint's literary career came to an abrupt conclusion. Alternatively we may suppose that he finished the book, but his housekeeper used the last page of it to light the fire, and he always told his friends that he would rewrite it one day, but he never did. Suppositions of this kind are easily made, but those who have played the game of history longest and hardest will probably agree that the fewer of them we have to make, the better it will be. So far as our evidence goes, St. Mark decided to end his gospel at verse eight of chapter sixteen.

But could he have done so? That is what learned men have asked themselves. I am not so much concerned with the proper answer to this question, as with the meaning of the question itself. If you say '*Could* he have taken his pen off the paper there?' what do you mean by 'could'? Some sort of a psychological difficulty, no doubt, is intended. *Could* he have felt that this was the proper place to stop? Well, why not? You cannot obviously mean 'He could not stop here, because things still went on happening after the women fled from the tomb'. Of course they did. History does not stop. St. Matthew, whose conclusion nobody cavils at, stopped short of the Ascension and Pentecost, though they are integral parts of the saving mystery. Nor can you mean 'He cannot stop yet, or he will have left us in ignorance of the principal thing, the Resurrection Christ', for those to whom he writes know about that in any case. Before their baptism they were taught the formula 'He rose again from the dead according to the Scriptures, and appeared first to Cephas, then to the Twelve'. Nor can you really mean (as is sometimes suggested) that he cannot stop yet, because his previous story contains hints of things still to be described, for example, St. Peter's restoration to grace. For this consideration proves too much: the gospel story contains hints of all sorts of future things which cannot in any case form part of its concluding narrative—the descent of the Spirit, the mission to the Gentiles, and the fall of Jerusalem. Nor is it a question of logic. If St. Mark is writing the history of Christ's earthly life, it is reasonable enough for him to end with his burial—an attempt was made to dispose of his body in the usual way, but when they came back to complete the funeral rites, it was no longer to be found— faith knows why. So ends the story of Christ's earthly life: what would follow would be the story of the Risen Christ and of the Church.

When we object that St. Mark could not end so, we mean none of these things. We mean that the conclusion lacks poetical inevitability, just that. In spite of our conventional sniffs at St. Mark for not writing grammarian's Greek, like Lucian of Samosata, we pay him an unconscious literary compliment; his supposedly artless story holds us as Lucian's artfulness never could (even if Lucian had ever had anything to say). St. Mark has built up in our mind strong poetic expectations: we feel them to be disappointed by his conclusion, and we cannot believe that such a writer could have written so ill.

The debate, then, is a literary debate: and if we try to defend the abrupt ending, we must do it by literary arguments. We must try to persuade ourselves that we have been missing the true poetic pattern of the book: either, like some of Mr. Eliot, it defeats us at first sight through our failure to pick up the crucial literary allusions; or we have been reading it through a haze of memories from St. Matthew and St. Luke, and not in its own clear light. The purpose of our arguments must be to show that the last line is inevitable in its finality—we must show that, so far from its being impossible for St. Mark to stop here, it would be impossible for him to go on.

I am not so foolish as to think that I can here and now make a decisive contribution to the controversy. But I shall say a

138

little more about it by way of illustration; I do not want you to be convinced that my argument is conclusive, I want to persuade you that it is the proper sort of argument for the purpose, and that it belongs to the *genre* of literary criticism.

What we desire to show is that the conclusion has poetical inevitability. The best way to suggest what this poetical inevitability would be, is to compose a short copy of verses which would give expression to it. Suppose we say something like this:

> '*Now walks Barabbas free, and Christ is bound.*
> *The sun is up: our hope is underground.*
> *Come, Mary Magdalen, Salome, come,*
> *With funeral odours grace the guarded tomb*'.
> *Seeking immortal Act among the dead,*
> *They heard his angel, trembled, turned, and fled.*

Now if you say to me 'Go on: give us another pair of rhymes to tell us what happened after that' I shall break all the strings of my lyre, and hang myself upon a willow tree.

My verses end where they do because, I hope, they have said what they set out to say. The act of God always overthrows human expectation: the Cross defeats our hope: the Resurrection terrifies our despair. Is this what St. Mark, also, wanted to say? It would not be surprising if it were. A theme which stands out as clearly as any other in his passion narrative is that no man knows what to do with the divine when it falls into his hands: we are reminded of the Philistines in uneasy possession of the Ark of the Covenant. A woman tries to anoint the Lord for glory, only to learn that she has fore-anointed him for burial. The apostles attempt heroics in defence of Christ, but when it comes to it they forsake him and flee, that he may remain and die for them. The priests condemn him to preserve their priesthood, but in condemning him they tear up their priesthood and overthrow their temple. Pilate crucifies him, falsely accused of claiming the earthly shadow of an eternal kingdom which is actually his.

The Arimathaean carefully buries him whom no sepulchre can hold, and the women, not understanding why his fore-anointing for burial with that festal nard had been providential, bring funeral myrrh to embalm the already risen God. The mere rustling of the hem of his risen glory, the voice of the boy in the white robe, turns them to headlong flight: 'and they said not a word to anyone, for they were afraid'. Do we stop there or do we go on? I think we stop.

This is to decide the question simply on the grounds of theme. Such a treatment cannot, of itself, be sufficient. We must judge it equally on the grounds of phrase.

'And issuing forth they fled from the sepulchre, for trembling and panic possessed them: and nothing did they say to any man, for they were afraid.' Has that the ring of finality? But in whose ear? Not in the ear of the student of Attic oratory, perhaps, or even the student of biblical Greek in general. But in the ear of the reader of St. Mark? St. Mark builds up his own rhythms, which gradually work themselves into our heads as we read his gospel through from the beginning. The element of rhythmic repetition is so obvious in this gospel that guileless critics have been led to see in it nothing but a string of spoken anecdotes, one reflecting the pattern of another with childish iteration. But the formal recurrences are St. Mark's poetical magic: one paragraph subtly echoes another, emphasizing persistent themes and throwing variations into relief.

Is it natural, upon this background, that the flight of disciples should provide a termination? Let us consider the parallel between two sections, one describing the last experiences of Jesus in the body at the hands of his disciples, the other describing the body of Jesus in the hands of his disciples after his death. The first section, which is much the longer, provides the following sequence:

When Jesus was at supper, a woman brought a jar of nard and anointed him: a good work, he said, for they would not have him always—she had fore-anointed his body for burial.

Presently Jesus is seen at supper again: he gives his disciples his sacramental body, and says to them: after I am risen again I will go before you into Galilee. In the garden he admonishes them—especially three of them—to watch, but they are taken unprepared by the catastrophe: all forsake him and flee, among them a youth in a linen cloth, who left it in his pursuer's hands to make good his escape.

The second sequence is this: Joseph obtains the body of Jesus from Pilate, and buries it, wrapping it in a linen cloth: three women bring perfumes to embalm it. Entering, they see a youth in a white stole. He bids them tell the disciples that Jesus goes before them into Galilee, as he had said to them (at the Supper). The women flee, saying nothing to anyone.

We may list the common features of the two sections. A woman in the one case, women in the other, come to perfume the body of Jesus: Jesus himself says that the first perfuming is what the second was intended to have been, a funeral anointing. In the first section Jesus prophesies that he will precede his disciples into Galilee: in the second the prophecy is explicitly recalled. In the first Jesus gives his disciples his sacramental body, which it really concerns them to have: in the second, disciples obtain and vainly wall up his physical body, which they are unable to keep. In both a symbolical part is played by a linen cloth—the youth in the garden is stripped of one, the sacred body is wrapped in one. The word 'linen cloth' is rare—St. Mark does not use it elsewhere. In both 'a lad' (again the word is confined to this pair of texts) 'clad in' some named garment plays a prominent part. In both a sudden catastrophe falls on disciples—the women at the sepulchre, the three special watchers in Gethsemane with their companions: and in both they react in the same way—by flight.

Of these points of comparison, the symbolism of the two linen cloths and of the two 'lads clad in' this or that attire may be completely opaque to us, but if we allow ourselves to neglect them for the present, we cannot be in any great doubt as to the sense attaching to the rest of the parallel. Jesus had said that the anointing at Bethany was—by anticipation—his burial-anointing: yet the women come and try to anoint him on the third day. Jesus had given his disciples his crucified body after a heavenly manner at the Supper, likewise by anticipation: yet they attempt to secure and reverence his crucified body after an earthly manner in the tomb. Jesus had promised them that he would be before them in Galilee; but here they are looking for his body outside the walls of Jerusalem. Jesus had many times forewarned them of the passion: he had as often promised them the Resurrection. The first breath of the approaching disaster caught them unprepared in the garden: the first sign of the dawning joy caught them unprepared at the tomb. The enemy's envoys grabbed a lad's shirt in the garden, and met in him and in the rest with no reception but headlong flight. The Saviour's envoy appeared as a lad in a robe at the tomb, and met with no reception from the women but headlong flight.

We see, then, that the firm ending to the Gethsemane episode prepares us to find a firm ending in the last words of the sepulchre episode. But we have not yet completed our task. 'Flight' is the last word in Gethsemane, and that seems a firm ending. But at the sepulchre 'they said not a word to anyone, for they were afraid' is the last word, an addition which may appear a weak ending. It may, so long as we confine our attention to the parallel we have so far drawn out. But the episode of the tomb, being the last in St. Mark's Gospel, may be expected to awaken echoes from many of the preceding pages, as well as from the narrative of Gethsemane. The narrative of the tomb is the last and greatest of the miracle-stories, and so it challenges comparison with the preceding stories, especially those of healing: for in his own resurrection Christ finally displays the principle of power by which he raised up the sick and the dead. We remember, then, how the healings of the ministry were again and again followed by popular proclamation, even though Christ enjoined silence. 'See that thou say nothing to any man,' said he to the leper: but the leper went forth and began to publish it much. Now at last the day for publication has come, and the women are tongue-tied. The angel said, 'Tell his disciples and Peter,' but they went forth and said nothing to any man, such was their fear.

The phrase about silence is therefore no weak addition or apologetic device: it keeps up the theme of human perversity to the last, and gives it its final expression. St. Mark is writing 'the Good Tidings of Jesus Christ, the Son of God', as his title declares. The Good Tidings are summed up in the Resurrection of the Son of God; now Christ is risen, and the gospel is laid upon the women's lips by his angel. But they 'said nothing to any man, for they were afraid'. St. Mark offers small comfort or support to believers in natural wisdom or virtue. Nothing earthly, not even Jesus in the flesh, not the healing touch of those blessed hands, or the divine persuasions of his tongue, not the spectacle of his passion or the angelic tidings of his resurrection, nothing but the Godhead of Jesus apparent in his risen being could lift men up to take hold of the life of God. Not until Peter and the rest were apprehended by the Lord of Glory in Galilee would they be made to stand, for Godhead itself would have come upon them, from which we can no more run than we can from the dawn. Then they would be made wise, and filled with the preaching. The message of an angel was not enough: the women ran from him, and were dumb.

In conclusion to this matter, we ought perhaps to say something of the linen winding sheet, the boy in linen, and the boy in a white robe. There is surely some symbolic motif here, if we could only hit upon it. It is not that there is anything inexplicable about the facts. In the scuffle at Gethsemane one disciple hit out with a sword before he ran: another left his coat in his pursuers' hands. Yet why does St. Mark trouble to mention it, and why (still more) does he trouble to tell us that it was 'fine linen?' Again, the Arimathean, burying Jesus' body, would of course wrap it: but why does St. Mark tell us so, and why does he specify the stuff as 'fine linen'? Again, all tradition knows that the women were met by an angelic vision, but where else in scripture is an angel described as 'a lad in a white robe'? Is not St. Mark turning his three phrases for the sake of allusion to one another? But if so, what is the point?

The confusion and flight of the disciples in Gethsemane is revealed as the natural effect of their failure to watch: they had fallen asleep, they could not watch one hour, so they fell into temptation. Now the priestly watchers in the temple who were caught sleeping on duty were beaten and had their robes taken from them; to which St. John makes allusion in his Revelation, when he is inspired to say in the name of Christ: 'Behold I come as a thief: blessed is he that watcheth and keepeth his garments, lest he walk naked and men see his shame.' Thus, the young man's loss of his linen coat is a dramatic symbol of the idea, 'Caught asleep on duty.' The sleeping guard, whose robe was snatched from him, was stripped of honour, and must slink naked away. The naked body of the crucified is wrapped in fine linen, to bestow honour upon it, and that its nakedness may not appear. It is part of the pathos of human burial that we bestow honour in vain on what must decay: it is part of the irony of the burial of Christ's body that men seek to wrap in the decency of funeral respect the flesh which God will immediately clothe with the radiance of glory, that mortality may be swallowed up in life. When the women come to anoint him whom Joseph had shrouded, he already wears the white stole of immortal being: his angel wears it when he gives the women his message. Those who fled from Gethsemane lost their honour; Joseph vainly sought to spread human honour upon the crucified; the angel in the tomb revealed the unspotted honour of heaven.

The three texts about the boy in the garden, Joseph's shrouding of Jesus, and the boy in the tomb, are held together by verbal echoes: they are also held together by the name of Joseph. The name of the Arimathean is remembered among so many names of minor persons forgotten, because it is significant. Joseph the Arimathean was indeed a Joseph, for as he had begged Pilate's permission to bury Jesus, so Joseph the patriarch had begged Pharaoh's permission to bury Israel, which cost him a troublesome journey. Now just as a Jew could not hear the story of a Joseph who fulfils the pious duty of burial under difficulties, without thinking of Joseph the patriarch, so he could not hear of a boy who leaves his coat in his captors' hands and escapes without thinking of the same patriarch; the story of Joseph and Potiphar's wife being a favourite moral tale for the instruction of the young. Thus, of our three allusions, two are Joseph-themes: but what of the third? Joseph was stripped, first by his eleven false brethren, then by Potiphar's wife: he was buried in prison and believed by the eleven to be dead. But in due course he appeared to them as though alive from the grave, clothed in a robe of glory as the man of the king's right hand: he said to them, 'I am Joseph.' But his brethren could not answer him, *for they were confounded.* Compare the women, confronted not, indeed, with the new Joseph in person, but with one who wears his livery, and unable to speak, *for they were afraid.* A glance at the Greek Old Testament will show the exactness of the verbal parallel. Joseph proceeded to overcome the shame and terror of the eleven who had sold him, and St. Mark's readers will know that Jesus is going, in Galilee, to overcome the shame and fear of the eleven who had deserted him: but to include that encounter within his gospel is a thing he cannot do: every sentence in the gospel points a finger towards it, but the poem ends with finality at the words 'for they were afraid'. The rest cannot be written.

We have discussed the ending of St. Mark, not to prove a thesis, but to show what sort of argument is appropriate. Such argument belongs plainly enough to the criticism of poetry, that is its *genre.* The further we go into the question, the more clearly we see that St. Mark's words are shaped by a play of images and allusions of the subtle and elusive kind which

belongs to imagination rather than to rational construction.
It may be, after all, that St. Mark's ending is not good poetry;
that there is a clumsiness about it, in spite of all we have said
in favour of it. But if it is imperfect poetry, it is still poetry,
and our dissatisfaction with it (if we still feel dissatisfaction) is
a poetical discontent.

The patterns of theme, phrase and symbol which we have
been examining in St. Mark do not put before us the sense and
substance of revealed truth. No one's salvation depends on the
comparison between Joseph with his eleven false brethren and
Jesus with his eleven cowardly disciples: or on the antique
symbolism of the robe of honour; or on the inverted parallels
which give opposite expression to the theme of human perversity. Do not let us suppose that these things are the substance of saving truth. The substance of the truth is in the
great images which lie behind, in the figure of the Son of
Man, in the ceremony of the sacramental body, in the bloody
sacrifice of the Lamb, in the enthronement of the Lord's
Anointed. What we have been looking at is a play of secondary images and ideas under the pressure of the great images.
Because the great images are alive and moving in the inspired
mind, the rhythm of secondary images is set in motion to be
their development and application. Through the secondary
images the force of the primary images is felt. The passion of
Christ will be more powerfully experienced through St.
Mark's poem than through the bare consideration of the
plain idea of it. The Christ of the passion speaks to us through
the very words: it is the words we must taste and meditate. If
we try to go round behind the words we have nothing but
theology, that is to say, nothing but dust and ashes. Theology
is an indispensible rule for reading the scriptures: it is not the
substance of the word of God.

Conclusions are not of much profit, or much interest—by
the time one comes to conclude one has said what is going to
be said; to conclude is only to say it again. In a course of
lectures such as this there is no sensational discovery saved up

for the last page—no last lightning flash of theological detection. But it may still be of use to correct the desultory movement of the exposition by drawing together certain of the themes into an ordered summary.

How does divine truth make itself apprehended by the human mind? Through what is highest, most central, most characteristic in the human mind, the understanding. Supernatural revelation extends the natural power of this faculty, it does not distort or supplant it. The understanding is wit and reason, no more the one than the other. Wit divines its object and begets a representation of it: reason disciplines the product of wit and works out its inspirations to a systematic construction. To know God by revelation man needs both reason and wit; without reason he could not make sense of revelation, without wit he could not receive it. It is the reception, not the interpretation of the revealed truth, which is the mystery: and so we have talked more of wit than of reason.

In what we call the ordinary operations of the mind the working of wit is mysterious enough, but it does not perplex us because we are accustomed to it. It is mysterious enough how wit proceeds when from signs of personal behaviour it divines and pictures another man's mind, or imagines upon indirect evidence the thought of a character in history. But we accept such inspirations without amazement, content with being able to identify the stimulus to which our wit has responded. Never mind how wit has worked, that is her own secret: but anyhow she was working upon the sense-perceptions we had of our neighbour's behaviour, or upon the written words which have descended to us from ancient authors. We are more consciously perplexed when we cannot see to what it is that wit has responded, as often happens in the case of the poet. His wit is creative invention, and yet it is not mere invention: it responds to what we vaguely call the character of human life. Somehow or other the symbol on which his mind fixes awakens unconscious echoes of memory in many levels of his mind, and through these the reality which first imprinted the memories controls the development of the poetic symbol, and makes it deeply and widely expressive.

In the case of divine inspiration the mystery is profounder still: the inspired mind projects images, but to what is it that the formation of the images responds? Not to any diffused sense of human life, but to the supernatural action of God. Christ, perhaps, we can conceive as simply the poet of his own active being, which he as directly knows as any poet knows the movement of his own natural mind. But to others, say to the apostles, the mystery of Christ is communicated by the overflow of Christ's Spirit upon them: what it communicates to them is nothing that they are, but a transcendent mystery which they no more than touch in the fine point of their own supernaturalized act.

Poetry and divine inspiration have this in common, that both are projected in images which cannot be decoded, but must be allowed to signify what they signify of the reality beyond them. In this respect inspiration joins hands with poetry, certainly, on the one side: but with metaphysical thinking on the other. Inspiration stands midway between the free irresponsibility of poetical images, and the sober and criticized analogies of metaphysical discourse. For metaphysics can express its objects in no other way than by images, but it pulls its images to pieces and strips them down in the exact endeavour to conform to the realities. Inspiration does not merely stand at a midway point between poetry and metaphysics; it actively communicates with both. The subjective process of inspiration is essentially poetical, the content it communicates is metaphysical. For inspiration teaches us about God, and God's existence is one of the mysteries which metaphysical discourse describes. Certainly, supernatural inspiration reveals about God what no natural metaphysicizing could ever apprehend. But what inspiration reveals, it reveals about God, so that the thought of the sheer deity of God is embedded in the revelation. To think this thought out is to enter on a metaphysical enquiry. Even if we do not think it out, the thought of sheer deity is still the raw material of metaphysics, that is to say, it belongs to the natural knowledge of God. Without it no supernatural revelation can be either received or understood.

If we take something from supernatural revelation and attribute it to natural reason we take nothing from God, for God is all. If we think we take anything from him we must suppose that we give it to another; but that other will also be he. Of all actions and effects he is the first originative cause. He has wonderfully ordained our natural state, and more wonderfully has redeemed it. Nature and divinizing grace are his alike, in both he is glorified, and more particularly in the compassion whereby he has grafted grace on our degenerated nature. But all is his. From the Father issues the Eternal Son, to be inbreathed with his co-equal Spirit, and from the three-fold fount of deity proceed all creatures, the manifold reflections of immortal love. *Therefore to the One God in Three Persons, Father, Son and Holy Ghost, be ascribed as is most justly due all might, dominion, majesty and power, henceforth and for ever.*

INDEX